GUIDED
Journaling

HOW TO USE AFFIRMATIONS, GRATITUDE & DAILY RITUALS TO MANIFEST, PRACTICE POSITIVITY AND CREATE A BALANCED LIFE

🐢 **Turtle**Publishing

Published by Turtle Publishing
All rights reserved.

Printed on demand in Australia, United States and United Kingdom.

Written & designed by Kathy Shanks
© Kathy Shanks 2021
Illustrations by Freepik Storyset & Turtle Publishing

Disclaimer: Please note the information contained within this document is for educational and entertainment purposes only. All effort has been executed to present accurate, up to date, and reliable, complete information. No warranties of any kind are declared or implied. Readers acknowledge that the author is not engaging in the rendering of legal, financial, medical or professional advice. The content within this book has been derived from various sources. Please consult a licensed professional before attempting any techniques outlined in this book.

ISBN (PRINT) 978-0-6452040-0-1
ISBN (eBOOK) 978-0-6452040-1-8

SPECIAL BONUS

FREE Guided Journaling Workbook to
help you begin journaling using some of
the techniques mentioned in this book.

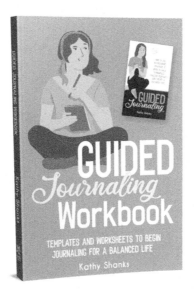

Get FREE unlimited access to this AND all of
my new books by joining our fan base!

SCAN WITH YOUR CAMERA OR GO TO
bit.ly/GuidedJournalingWorkbook

TABLE OF CONTENTS

ABOUT THE AUTHOR

Kathy Shanks is a businesswoman and entrepreneur, as well as a wife of 18 years and a mother of two. She has been self-employed for over twenty years and started three businesses from the ground up. She sold one during COVID's peak, and she is still managing the other two.

Not only that, but Kathy is unbelievably passionate about the power of developing self-belief through journaling. She is a firm believer that anyone can do anything they set their mind to. For Kathy, there is no such thing as failure. You just keep on trying and trying until what? It gets done. Then, you set another goal. Life is a journey of constantly building goals. That applies to work life, personal life, and inner life.

Many years ago, while attending a very intense personal development event, she was incredibly inspired to make some changes in her life. It was the sort of content that gives you that 'light-bulb moment' we always hear about. She thought to herself, *why did I not hear this 20 years ago?* As she was thinking this, the lady who was sitting next to her said, "I wish I'd heard this 20 years ago."

Kathy looked up at her for the first time since they'd entered the room. Her mind was blown for the second time in as many minutes. The lovely lady who felt the need to say this out loud was approximately 20 years older than her. A few things hit Kathy all at once. Firstly, she realised with relief that she still had time. Secondly, the reality is that she probably did hear something like this 20 years ago. But she wasn't ready to really 'hear' it and take it on board. Thirdly, she wondered, *what am I not hearing now that perhaps in 20 years I wish I had listened to?*

Since then, Kathy has filled her mind with as much personal development content as her brain could handle. She loves learning new things, but she wanted more than just the information. She wanted to take action. That's when she started developing her own method of journaling. She started creating a system that would bring together her love of journaling, her skills as a graphic designer, and all the information she'd collected from others' success.

You can imagine how tricky this was to fit this in along with managing businesses and family commitments whilst maintaining a healthy balanced life. But all her efforts collected to create this book you have in front of you. These are the tools and methods that Kathy has built, creating her own journaling style that she wants to share with YOU. It's only a matter of you taking the initiative to get started. Are you ready?

Then let's go. Time to learn about journaling, how it works, why it works, and how you can use it to build your best possible life.

PART ONE

The Foundations of Journaling

CHAPTER ONE

The possibilities are endless

"Writing is an exploration. You start from nothing and learn as you go." – E.L. Doctorow

Who are you? Do you feel like you know the answer to that question? Do you feel that you get to express all parts of your personality? Or do you feel something is missing in yourself or your life? Have you ever felt frustrated about your relationships, your career, or just the way you see the world? Perhaps you are a great mum, a talented employee, an entrepreneur, or a health nut. But, do you feel like you excel in one part of your life and come up short in the others?

You may have considered journaling before, but have you *really* made an effort to use it to help improve your life? What you're about to learn will help you go deeper into your journaling. It'll help you define the areas of your life that you want to delve into more. It'll help you use a long-standing process (writing things down on paper) to really hone in on what you want, when you want it, and how you're going to work towards it. It'll help you start to create a thought process that not only improves your every day (right now), but also a process that can manifest your wildest dreams. All great stories start with a dream, a 'one-day' where the future will be brighter. Organising your thoughts and dreams in 10-20 minutes a day can be that one simple change that actually makes those dreams become a reality.

You know what journaling is. You've seen it in action: pen, little notebook, someone tucked away in a corner scribbling words out. Perhaps that someone was even you. But it's possible that you don't know the variety or scope of what journaling can actually do for you.

Everyone has days when they wake up and just want to turn off the alarm and stay in bed. That's normal. But is that the way you want to live your life? Wouldn't you rather open your eyes and smile with wonder at all the things that could happen during your day? That's not only possible but probable when you discover how gratitude and affirmations can change the way you look at your life from the second you open your eyes to the moment you close them at night.

Do you find yourself imagining a different life, a different job, different relationships as you go about your day? Perhaps you imagine living somewhere else, doing different work, or even retiring early. *Just dreams*, you think to yourself. But they can be more than dreams. You can get what you wish for, but it takes work.

It takes effort to work on yourself and get over those hurdles that hold you back from being where you want to be. You can't reach those dreams until you genuinely believe that you deserve them and that they are within your reach. As long as you think that they are only dreams and that you are not capable of making them happen, they will remain dreams.

To reach a dream, you must believe in yourself. Journaling begins this process of creating self-belief. It's a process of switching our brains to a new path, and creating a belief in ourselves that we are actually worthy of what we seek. If you don't think you are worthy, then you'll never get to where you want to go. Once you understand that you are worthy of your dreams, then your dreams can become a reality.

The focus of this book is diverse. It's about developing **gratitude** through journaling. It's about creating **daily rituals** that give you a feeling of contentment and happiness for all aspects of your life. And, it's also about **manifesting** the *future you* that you have always wanted to be. These skills do not come overnight. They may not come for a long time. They can, however, become a 'new' normal if you find time to practice journaling each day.

If you have never tried journaling, you might be hesitant to get started. That's understandable. People who haven't journaled can easily become overwhelmed by all the information that is out there. How do you know which journaling style is right for you? How do you find the time? How do you know what to journal about? How do you actually go about 'journaling'?

One of the best things about journaling is that there is no wrong way to do it. This is **your** journey. It's all about you. You can take the information in this guide and use it in a way that suits your lifestyle. You can adapt it to suit your personality. It's not another how-to book that will leave you wondering why you wasted your money on something that you can't possibly fit into your life because this guide can work in anyone's life. It's all about **you**.

This journaling guide is for anyone that has felt frustrated about their relationships, their career, or just the way they see the world. If you feel like there are more negative than positive things in your life, you will benefit from this book.

You might not use every trick or idea listed, and that's completely okay. Use whatever works best for you to get started on your path. Take a strategy here and there if that's what works for you! The future belongs to you, and this is only step one.

Chapter Summary

To sum up...

- This journaling guide is for anyone that has felt frustrated about their relationships, their career, their health, or just the way they see the world.

- Have you considered making a real effort towards journaling? To really dive deep to help in all areas of your life?

- Reaching your dream life requires self-belief.

- This book is all about developing gratitude, daily rituals, and manifesting the *future you*.

- There is no right or wrong way to journal. This is your journey. It's about finding what's suitable for you.

In the next chapter, you will learn what journaling is. You'll get a **broad picture** of what the journaling process entails and the different types of journaling that people use to make progress in their lives. Remember, find the right style that works for you.

CHAPTER TWO

The journaling rundown

"What a comfort is this journal. I tell myself to myself and throw the burden on my book and feel relieved." - ***The Secret Diaries of Anne Lister***

Now, most likely, you know what journaling is in general. We all have an idea of what we think journaling is, but it's many things to many people... some of which may surprise you.

Types of Journaling

A common question about journaling is, "how do you do it effectively, or in a way that makes you want to keep going back for more." The answer to this is really simple - **whatever way that inspires you, fulfils you, and makes YOU want to keep going.** What if you don't want to sit down with a notepad and a pen and write? Then don't. For some people, doing it the traditional way is the best option. But this doesn't work for everyone.

There are so many resources out there for journaling. Choose whatever works for you and your lifestyle! Often, people don't get into journaling because they don't like sitting down and writing in a notebook. But you can do journaling in any way! The benefits are the same.

Let's discuss some of the ways you can journal.

The Old Stand-By (a trusty notebook and pen)

In general terms, journaling is the practice of writing in a notebook. Do people still do this? The answer to that question is "yes." It's still a very common practice around the world. Traditional journaling is a time for you to sit down and write how you're feeling, why you feel that way, as well as a record of what you've done. This is also called a diary.

Prompt Journaling

Prompt journaling is another strategy used and has become very popular in recent times. It's similar to the traditional journal in the sense that it requires a notebook and pen. It differs though, in the way that you are given prompts to make journal entries. There are many types of prompt journals available - gratitude journals, health journals, goal setting journals, happiness journals, affirmation journals, self-love journals - the list is endless.

These can be particularly helpful in focusing your journaling strategy. If you struggle with the idea of what to put in a blank journal, prompt journals are ideal.

Bullet Journaling

You've probably heard of bullet journaling and seen all of the amazing Pinterest photos. They can look quite artistic and be mesmerising to look through. Bullet journaling is a blank book where you can schedule all your day-to-day activities plus your goals and to-do lists all in one place. These are particularly well suited to creatives who enjoy spending time making their journals look amazing, but can also suit non-creatives who want a structured journal that is completely their own. It's a form of prompt journaling that you design. These can be very time-consuming, but once researched and started, you can bring your journaling back to 10-20 minutes per day.

Art Journaling

Perhaps you're a more visual person? An art journal is your own private space that can allow you to draw and be creative while exploring your thoughts and feelings. You can use a combination of words, images, colours and patterns. It differs from a sketchbook in that you are creating images of your innermost thoughts and ideas.

Voice Recordings

Maybe you prefer to record yourself rather than spend time writing things out. You could use many voice-to-text apps to create a document of your verbal thoughts, or you could simply keep your recordings.

Use a Journaling App

There's an app for everything. You can use one to write down your thoughts and everything you feel is important. There's sure to be an app to suit your needs. And, the best part? It's on your phone and laptop and can be taken anywhere with you. It's private for your eyes only. There are plenty of journaling apps you can find that you can use on your phone or iPad. Journaling on the go!

Write a Blog

Maybe you want to share your thoughts with people that you think you could help! Then, blogging could be a good way for you to go! You can set up your blogging site, create a pen name and get started. There's a method for everyone, and it's all journaling. Sometimes, people just prefer typing. And it can be a speedier way to get down your thoughts.

Reasons for Journaling

People turn to journaling for many reasons.

Self-Discovery

One of the biggest reasons that people start to keep a journal is to learn more about themselves. Self-discovery can be a scary path to go down, but it can make a massive difference to how you view the world around you. A journal is a reflection zone. You can use it to write about yourself in general and how things are going in your life. You might begin to find patterns as you go along: emotions or issues that keep coming up that need resolving, or even positive things you're doing that you didn't even realise.

Life Changes

Perhaps you may start to write in a journal to help you through a difficult time in your life. Journaling can be a very therapeutic. The loss of a loved one, the break-up of a relationship, living in a new town or city, or even a change in career. All of these things can be challenging and force us to think differently about our lives. A journal can be a safe place to write about all the emotions that are going on inside you. It's a place where you can unburden yourself and gather your thoughts.

Mental Health

Journaling can have a massive impact on your mental health. It may help you de-stress, be a better problem-solver, give more clarity with your thoughts, and resolve any disagreements. Journaling can be such a cathartic relief that therapists will often encourage their patients to do so. Research has shown that just sitting down and writing down your thoughts for fifteen or twenty minutes helps patients deal with traumatic stress and emotions. It acts as a listener when nobody else will. And the best thing? It's there, strictly to benefit you, nobody else!

Talking to someone always helps, but journaling is a great resource when you feel like you can't speak to anyone else. Sharing your emotions is important, and you shouldn't hold strong feelings in. Journaling is your chance to begin the healing process of unburdening whatever is weighing you down. It can make you feel like there's a listening ear, especially when you feel you don't have anyone else to turn to.

What you journal about is completely up to you, but some common themes are your health, gratitude you feel in everyday life, your feelings, a current state of mind, the love you feel, or the evaluation of your emotions. The most common reason people journal is to process emotions such as fear, anger, or frustration, to name a few.

Writing these kinds of things down can help to release feelings of frustration, anxiety, or stress. Instead of feeling bombarded, you can take a deep breath and start writing. Journaling helps you to control your emotions and understand your feelings better. In our minds, things can seem a bit jumbled. But looking at your words all written down in a journal can help you feel a little bit more organised and less frenzied. To put it simply, journaling can make the world seem like a much clearer place.

Creating Balance

We are not just talking in vague, flowery terms, journaling really does make a difference. The act of journaling can assist in creating balance in your life. Do you ever feel so overwhelmed, like you have so much going on, but you can't get through it all? Journaling can help you with that and more. There's no need for you to panic because you think you have too much on your plate. This method will let you sort through these thoughts, so you can 'tidy-up' your mind and find the best way to get through them.

In order to live a healthy and happy life, balance is important. You can't work so much on your business that you neglect to spend time with your family. And, the opposite can also be said. You can't hang out with your friends so much that you're not getting work done, and, all of a sudden, your bills aren't being paid. It's so important to work on all aspects of your life, and journaling can help you with that.

I've always been a list-maker. I would have lists of to-do's and lists in my lists to make my lists more organised. This was how I created organisation in my life—getting all the parts of my life down on a piece of paper was like physically removing them from my head. I would instantly feel calm again. The many thoughts in my head were accounted for in one of those lists. Keeping these plans in your journal and actively working towards them can help you succeed in all parts of your life.

Working Towards a Better Life

Everybody thinks about the future, some people more than others. How you envisage your future is entirely up to you, but journaling can help you. By acknowledging your current state and creating a plan for the future, you can see how you can achieve it. You can start taking steps to achieve that future. You can mould it whatever way you want to create a future that you're happy with using manifesting and affirmations.

Manifest your best life by creating and developing new internal beliefs. Like we mentioned in chapter one, you need to believe that you are worthy of what you seek. That's what manifesting is. Believe in what you will achieve, and you can make it happen. In order to help manifest, you can work on 'as if' journaling, where you write out a day in the life that you hope for. Maybe it's describing a day at work in your dream job or a holiday with your new partner.

Journaling affirmations that manifest is a very powerful tool indeed. Affirmations are often thought of as statements that are short, powerful, and pack a punch. They are supposed to have a strong impact when thought of or said out loud. Manifesting and affirmations are linked in that we can create new internal beliefs using affirmations. Both are key elements in journaling for your future and will be discussed in further chapters.

An Educational Tool

If that's not enough for you, let's look at this from a knowledge standpoint. Journaling can be a learning tool. It's often recommended apprentices track what they do and the reasons for their actions. Journaling allows you to not just look over your actions but to analyse them. By doing this, you can re-evaluate your decisions and efforts and improve yourself. This allows you to reach your future goals.

Benefits of Journaling

The journaling process can reap many benefits when you commit to it. If you make time for yourself and your journal each day, you can discover some of the many benefits:

- **Emotions.** Uncover feelings and emotions that you didn't even know were there and could tell you a lot about yourself and how you operate.

- **What's holding you back.** Journaling can help you see patterns in your behaviour and may help you understand that there is something that has been holding you back from reaching your highest potential. Once you know what it is, you can deal with it.

- **Anxiety.** Do you ever have anxious feelings that leave you overwhelmed and unmotivated? Left unchecked, anxiety can lead to more serious things, such as stress and trauma. By working through these, you can stop these feelings before they progress by minimising them and getting rid of them. Journaling can be an escape for you by expressing your feelings by documenting them down on the page.

- **Depression.** You won't get cured of depression just because you journal, but you can receive a multitude of benefits by adding it to your daily schedule. Journaling has been recommended to improve your mood and manage the symptoms that you may be feeling. Through the ups and downs, it can become a constant for you.

- **Stress.** Everyone experiences stress, but how you deal with it is one aspect of what makes you, you. You can use journaling to examine your thoughts and feelings to find out what's making you stressed out in the first place. Then, you can release these emotions and get rid of any negative thoughts and feelings that you may be feeling.

- **Mental Health.** As mentioned before, journaling can help to understand what you may be feeling. By journaling, you can prioritise your problems and concerns and why they weigh down on you. By doing this, it may allow you to recognise what triggers your thoughts and feelings, and then figure out better ways of managing them.

- **Sleep.** What are some things that keep you up all night? Journaling can help you to reduce these emotions. How? By setting aside fifteen minutes every night, you can write about a positive experience and how it made you feel, increasing how much you sleep and improve your sleep quality. Think gratitude. If thoughts and feelings still keep you awake at night, keep a journal beside your bed so you can write them down. Instead of tossing and turning, you can get them out of your head and onto paper.

- **Focus.** By forcing you to slow down and reflect, journaling helps you to have better focus. Sometimes we're so busy 'doing life' we don't have time to reflect on the big picture. Journaling allows you to focus on what you *really* want, away from the chaos.

- **Staying motivated.** Simply writing down your goal is the first step to recognising what you want and achieving it. Writing it sends the goal through your left hemisphere, the logical side, which makes you more likely to work towards earning it.

- **Cohesive heart.** Have you ever felt that your thoughts are different from what your heart says? That the two are constantly battling against each other? Journaling can help you reconcile the difference between what your heart wants, and what your head knows.

- **Discover your gratitude.** And gratitude is the secret to a happy life.

Imagine waking up each day and opening your eyes to a sense of gratitude. You don't even have to have a specific person, event, or thing in mind that you are grateful for. You just know that there **will** be something that you feel grateful for in your day, and that gives you the positive attitude you need to get out of bed and manifest goodness in your day.

Essentially, for me, journaling is all about discovering your gratitude. You can reflect on what you have with gratitude, and you can manifest what you want with gratitude. You can also be grateful for the process of change and the results that you receive. Everything you're about to learn comes back to developing gratitude.

Gratitude does not come easily, and for most of us, it doesn't come naturally. Not at first anyway. Gratitude takes **practice**. Seeing things that you are grateful for comes more easily when you put effort into looking for them each day.

The beautiful part of the journaling process is that it creates a habit of looking at your life through fresh and open eyes. Once that habit is created, it becomes easy. You might even find this time will become your most peaceful and happy part of your day.

Chapter Summary

To sum up...

- Journaling can be with a blank notebook, prompted journal, you could use an app, record your voice, or an online document. It's up to you! Make journaling suit your lifestyle.

- Journaling just to get out feelings is limiting all the benefits you can reap from journaling. It also can be used for planning, self-discovery, organisation, and gratitude.

- Journaling can help reduce anxiety, stress, and aid with mental health, sleep and focus.

- The secret to happy life is gratitude. Developing gratitude is a skill that can be built with journaling.

In the next chapter, you will learn about how to work towards achieving that desired **life balance**. Journaling is the way to help you figure out where you're contributing your energy and focus, and how to spread it evenly to get that beautiful balance.

CHAPTER THREE

Work towards balance

*"Time and balance the two most difficult things to have control over, yet they are both the things that we do control." - **Catherine Pulsifer***

In this book, we're focusing on journaling to create a balanced life. In chapter two, you learned a little bit about why balance is important. Now, we're going to delve further into it to give you a better and clearer understanding. This is all about creating a sense of harmony and balance and maintaining it in your everyday life.

Have you ever really stopped to think about whether or not your life was balanced? It's a weird question to ask yourself, but it's an important one. In life, you need to have a median, a balance between all of the different aspects that you have. You see balance or lack of balance all around us in our everyday lives. For example, if you never exercise or eat healthily, your body will lose its strength and vitality. But if you starve yourself or work out too much, then you become brittle or injured. You need to find that sweet spot. This applies to so many areas of our lives.

Let's break this down into five important aspects of life.

Matters of the Heart

Journaling for the heart is all about taking time just for you to give yourself what you need to feel fulfilled. What's something that you like to do that is just for your own benefit? What makes you shine on the inside and feel happy? This can be as simple as writing affirmations, crazy dancing like nobody's watching, walking with a friend or going for a run with your own thoughts.

What are your beliefs? How do you nurture these? Is it through your religion, meditation or yoga that you fill your heart space? Whatever you do, your spiritual side can have a massive influence on different areas of life and especially how you view yourself and your place in the world.

Do you do something just for yourself that can make you feel better when you're having a bad day? Time for self-nurturing and reflection can affect your mood.

Perhaps you don't know what it is that you need to do for your heart, but journaling and creating new rituals can put you on the path of self-discovery. Use this time to discover what fills your heart.

Managing your Health

Your health is a huge deal because it dictates other aspects of your life. Have you ever noticed that when you're feeling healthy, you're more willing to do things that have to be done rather than when you may be feeling tired or rundown?

Managing your health encompasses both your physical and your mental health. They're equally important, and neither is above the other. Your health should be prioritised because it's essentially the decision-maker in life. It's at the helm, steering all other aspects. Without the management of health, many other areas of our life are more challenging.

Feeding your Mind

It's essential to continually grow our knowledge and our mindset. Anthony J. D'Angelo said,

> *"Develop a passion for learning. If you do, you will never cease to grow."*

You're going to change throughout your life. Your life circumstances will change as you get older. The people you spend time with will change. You can choose how you feed your mind throughout these changes to become the version of you that you want to become. You aren't an unwilling participant in your life. You guide the ship. Through your decisions, you create the life you lead, and it's through knowledge, you can make better decisions. You can choose to educate yourself in specific areas of your work, your mindset, how you express yourself, and so much more. Use your journaling to pursue interests, explore ideas and remind yourself to feed your mind regularly.

Nurturing Relationships

We all have important relationships in our lives. Romantic partners, family, friendships, and other relationships can all be very rewarding. They can act as a great de-stressor and a relaxer. Making time for all varieties of relationships brings a lot of joy and laughter into your life, however, it's easy to ignore their importance.

Relationships aren't always fun and games either. Journaling can help when they are harmful and problematic. It's a great way to resolve any internal issues you are struggling with. Gratitude can be a fantastic assistant with these challenges.

Creating a Life Mission

Whatever you do in your life to make a living or contribute to the world is important. It doesn't have to be a big grand dream. It can be simply seeking more fulfilling employment that allows you to help children in need.

Perhaps you do have big career aspirations, plan to start your own business, or create a charity. The amount of time you work can change the different aspects of your life because it can dictate how much time you spend with your family or working on your health. It's so important that you don't overwork yourself. And the same can be said for the opposite. Underworking yourself is just as problematic. Money is vital in your day-to-day life. It's essential to survival! It would be best if you were making enough money to live comfortably so that you're not stressing yourself out. But as necessary as this is, it also cannot be the sole purpose of why you're living

Our life mission is often a part of our 'big picture' goals, which can mean that we put it aside to manage day-to-day tasks. Journaling with life mission in mind, allows us to work towards our goals whilst still managing a balance in our lives.

***

All five of these aspects need to be considered when trying to figure out how to bring balance to your life. If you focus on just one thing, just one aspect, then you're putting all of your energy into that, which can be very unhealthy. If you spread your focus to different parts of your life, you'll create a more balanced life for yourself.

Let's relate this to journaling. When you're journaling using whichever method or strategy you choose, it's important to focus on all life aspects. If you only focus on one aspect, you create an imbalance that leads you to think only about one or two aspects of your life and leave the others to rot or remain stagnant.

For example, if you journal only about your future goals, then your personal relationships may suffer. When you put all of your focus towards one goal, that's where you're going to succeed the most. In order to properly succeed through life, first, start with journaling about the different aspects, and, in return, you'll be forced to divide your focus among them, leading to a more balanced life.

How can you create balance in your journaling? You don't have to write about each aspect every day, but you could do weekly or monthly overviews of them. By doing this, you can see whether your life is balanced or not. Download the free guided journal included with this book to start using this method.

Let's start with the health aspect. When you're trying to live a balanced life, it's increasingly important that you take care of yourself. Although this sounds like it's something simple that everyone knows, you will benefit from breaking this down. How are your eating habits? Do you eat out a lot or stay at home and cook? How much do you sleep at night? When was the last time that you exercised? These are all questions that you may ask yourself.

Do you know the answers to those questions? And, if you don't, it's because you might not be taking the best care of yourself, which means you're not living a balanced life. By keeping a journal, you can track these habits and adjust them accordingly.

Taking care of yourself should be one of your priorities. However, what are some of your other priorities? Maybe you just got a new job, or perhaps you're starting a family. Regardless of what stage of life you're in, it's still important that you prioritise. Journaling can help you stop biting off more than you can chew.

Another big part of creating balance, is simply managing your state of mind. When we have a lot going on, it is difficult to be calm and feel in control. If we're constantly worried or feeling like our life is chaotic, it's challenging to enjoy the small moments in life. One step towards creating this state of calmness can be to create more efficiency in your life. If you're struggling to keep up with everything, evaluate what you're doing with journaling. Are you sleeping in too late and feel like you're rushing around? Maybe, you spend so much of your time out with friends that you hardly have time for anything else? Perhaps your self-talk is so negative you're making yourself miserable?

Maybe you could use your journal as a planner. Take time every day, or every week, to write down precisely what you should be doing. Plan out your work commitments, recreational activities, study goals and time with friends and family. Use your journal to stay ahead of the game.

Spend time using your journal to work through each of the aspects and see what areas need to be worked on. When you have these thoughts written down, there's nothing that can stop you from doing them except yourself.

Do you have to write about all aspects of your life right from the beginning? Of course not. Maybe you just want to write about a few of the important ones you tend to forget about or throw aside. And that's completely fine. The most important thing that you have to remember about journaling is the fact that it's meant for you. Do whatever works best for you.

Chapter Summary

To sum up...

- Balance is everything. It's the difference between feeling energised and burnt out, happy and unhappy, fulfilled and unfulfilled.

- Focus on the five aspects of life when thinking about balance. Reflect on where your life might be a little imbalanced.

- Create balance in your journaling. Don't just focus on one aspect only in your journal, or all your progress and energy will go to that. Spread out your focus to all the areas.

- You can start small. One can't adjust their life imbalance all at once because it's a lot to tackle. However, your journal is the key.

In the next chapter, you will learn about those magic phrases called **affirmations**. If you're struggling with how to get your journal started, then this next chapter will be your ticket. Affirmations can give you a stepping stone and a map to the future that has always seemed just out of reach.

CHAPTER FOUR

Use affirmations to uplevel

*"There is nothing either good or bad but thinking makes it so." – **William Shakespeare***

Before you can journal to create balance in your life, you need to understand what affirmations are and why they are important. Affirmations are **powerhouse** statements. What do you think of when you read the word 'powerhouse'? Something strong, unshakeable? Something that holds its own? Something that can't be stopped? Those are the same traits of affirmations.

Affirmations are referred to as positive thinking and self-empowerment statements. They are short, simple expressions that evoke strength and confidence, not unlike mantras. Using affirmations supports a positive mentality that will help you to succeed.

Affirmations can help our mental state in innumerable ways:

- They can change the way you think, feel, and behave
- They can tear down old ways of thinking and help create new, positive ones
- They can fill you with positive energy as opposed to debilitating negative energy
- They can help you form a new path of thinking, thus affecting a new way of life

Thousands upon thousands of thoughts flit through our minds every day. They range from meaningless to painful to intriguing to positive. We can't stop them. They come and go, and that's just a fact of life. What if we could change the **way** we think to bring a positive, meaningful change in our lives?

Have you ever felt like something was holding you back from achieving your dreams? Something that was stopping you from becoming the very best that you can be? Perhaps it's you stopping yourself, and you don't even realise it? There will always be negativity in your life, whether from yourself or others or the world, but how you choose to react is the way you can fight back.

Affirmations are a way to battle against the negative thoughts that occupy your mind. When you're trying something new, you're sure to have had thoughts like, *I can't do it* or *I won't be as good as they are*. That's negativity hard at work in your mind, and your job is to fight against it by using affirmations. That way, you can build a path to a better, more positive life.

Some common affirmations that you need more of in your life:

- I am enough
- I believe in myself and my dreams
- I am whole and complete
- I am blessed with an incredible family and wonderful friends
- I am the architect of my life and my path
- I have all the qualities I need to have a successful life
- I am strong. I will defeat...

The list is practically endless! You can find multiple, effective affirmations with the click of a mouse, and you can make them your own. Twist them until they fit the words you want to remind yourself each and every day.

While it's important to say them to yourself in your mind each day, it's even more powerful to **write** them down. Similar to taking notes in a class, writing helps make connections in your subconscious mind. Not only can you write down your affirmations and keep them in visible places around your house, but you can journal them too!

Suppose you don't want to use 'stock' affirmations, no worries! You can create your own, and that will make them even more suitable to you, your needs, and the path you want to go on. But there are a few things to remember. In order to create solid, effective affirmations, you need to use strong statements.

Start your affirmations with phrases like 'I am', 'I can', or 'I will'. Don't get tied up with useless affirmations that begin with 'I'll try' or 'I might'. No! You want your affirmations to be **powerful** and **confident**, pulling your mind towards the knowledge that you can succeed at what you set your mind to. It doesn't have to be something you **might** get around to doing if you feel so inclined.

It's easy to feel a little shy in the face of such powerhouse statements. You might be thinking:

- *Can I really achieve this?*
- *That's scary, I don't think I can do it.*
- *What if I don't get there?*
- *I know I won't make it; what's the point of even trying?*

Those kinds of thoughts are perfectly normal, yet they can be damaging. A high percentage of us suffer from **'imposter syndrome'**. It sounds strange, but it's surprising how many of us can relate to such a feeling. Imposter syndrome is the belief that we aren't deserving of what we achieve. It's feelings of inadequacy even though success surrounds us. We might achieve something great or even be recognised for it, and yet we hold back from celebrating our achievements. We might feel like we don't deserve such an award. We're actually a fraud, and someone is eventually going to find us out.

This feeling could stem from a lot of areas. Perhaps you were labelled as 'the funny one' in your family, and you've never seen yourself as anything else. The Greek philosopher Aristotle once said,

> *"Give me a child until he is 7 and I will show you the man."*

Studies have proven that the ages 0-7 hold some importance in a child developing social skills. No matter our upbringing, many of us have labels and beliefs from this age that we can find hard to escape. Perhaps we dare to step outside of that label and achieve something, but we then feel uncomfortable with that achievement. We feel like our success is fraudulent, and it won't last. And just like that, our happiness and contentment are stolen from us simply from a bad headspace that we're in.

Think of your mind like a trash basket. Things fall into it, and you are holding it in your hands. Like meditation, you don't have to stop thoughts at the doorway to your brain and not allow them entry. You can let them flow in, but just as quickly send them back out again. Look down at the trash basket and see what's gone into it. And then pick through it.

Remove the useless thoughts, the ones that don't serve you in achieving your goals for the future. Keep the ones that do. While the process sounds simple, the implementation may take some time. But that's what affirmations are for. To give you a rock to stand on as you face the future you want to have.

In part two of this book, you will learn a process you can use to prepare your journaling method for each aspect of your life. There are four steps – *Reflect, Dream, Bridge the Gap and Decide*. During the third step, *Bridge the Gap*, you will reflect on where you are in life now, where you wish you could be, and figure out how you can bridge this gap. During this phase, consider the person you need to become to live your dream life. It is here that you can consider the affirmations that will serve you the best. For example, if you want to become an influential podcaster, but the reality is you feel you aren't influential enough, you can create affirmations to build this belief. 'I am inspirational'; 'I am educated'; 'I am worthy of success.' Sometimes 'bridging the gap' isn't about doing anything except believing that you deserve the dream. This is where affirmations can become your most powerful ally.

Imagination is a powerful thing, but writing is also a powerful tool. Write it down on the page. You can see it there in front of you: your future, ready for you to work toward. Uplevel yourself and manifest your future. Take control of your life and stop being victim to the cruel hands of fate. Negativity surrounds us every day. It fills our world. However, we don't need to let it creep into our minds and hearts and steal away a beautiful life and future.

Think of this scenario. A woman in her mid 30's has achieved a lot in her career. She has followed her dream and achieved what she wanted to achieve. But there are those in her life that wish to tear her down. She might have had a nasty divorce, leaving her feeling spent, useless, guilty, or even resentful. She could have fierce competitors in her line of work who choose to tear her down at any chance they get, and she feels like she constantly has to watch her back. Or perhaps even her parents are not supportive of her dreams or often try to label her as the child they once knew.

Each day, this woman feels drained, fatigued, and pointless. She sees her success, but it doesn't give her any pride or happiness. She is constantly dragged or weighed down by the constant demands on her or the negative energy of others. She wakes up each day filled with dread at what negativity she might face at work or elsewhere. Her heart and mind aren't filled with beautiful gratitude.

This doesn't sound like a peaceful life, does it? However, it's one we may all find familiar. Life is a crazy grouping of events, and not all of them are nice ones. So, it's up to us to make the difference. What if this woman took steps to change her life simply by journaling using affirmations?

Each day, she could wake up, focused on the affirmation: *I am strong. I deserve positive things in my life.* She pencils it in her journal each day and writes about the kinds of changes she wants to see in her life. She wants to appreciate her success. She wants to cut out the negative people in her life or detach her emotions from them. With each day, she grows stronger.

The repetitive nature of affirmations gets you to believe in them. To believe in yourself. Just like living in a negative world repeatedly being told something negative sucks you in, affirmations can do the same. But in contrast, they work to build you up again.

After a few months of working hard towards her goals, this woman starts waking up with a smile on her face. She sees the bright sunshine and the potential of each day. She enjoys time with her journal every morning to work on her affirmations and write down what positive things she sees or wants to see. In regards to her job, she's grateful for her success.

She may continue to win awards or be singled out for praise, and she doesn't have to turn it away, feeling shameful anymore. She is no longer an 'imposter'. People may still come and try to tear her down, but she doesn't listen to them any longer. She's not attached to their harmful words because she knows the truth now. She keeps working hard, living the life she wants to live, knowing inside of herself that she deserved what good things happened to her. She is strong.

Believe it: Journaling using affirmations can do the same for you. Wherever you might be in life, it can pull you out of that funk and push you forward. To use the old adage, *there is light at the end of the tunnel.* Even if it's faint or even if you don't think you can see it, it's there! Think of affirmations and journaling as your oil and your engine to start you off, riding out in the distance towards a happier, more successful, and satisfying future.

Chapter Summary

To sum up...

- Negativity is all around us. But it's how we react to it that can make the change and keep us from sinking deeper.

- Affirmations are short, expressive statements that instil confidence and power.

- Thinking is powerful. Use affirmations to change thinking and build a path to a better future.

- Use affirmations in your journaling to uplevel yourself and reach a future that you always dreamed of.

- Affirmations are your oil, and journaling is your engine to propel you toward a better, happier future. All you need to do is take that first step.

In the next chapter, you will learn how to **manifest** that *future you* that you've wanted to become for so long. You know it: it IS possible.

CHAPTER FIVE

Manifest the 'future you'

"Ask for what you want and be prepared to get it." – **Maya Angelou**

Manifesting: it's the hot word bouncing around talk shows, podcasts, and the internet in general. Everyone is talking about it. But what does it actually mean? Manifesting is about taking what you want and making it **real**. It's about creating success by believing that you can achieve your dreams.

The problem is that many think that manifesting is just a bunch of people saying what they desire or want to achieve, and that's the end of it. It's just a matter of stating your goals, and then you will somehow miraculously achieve them by sitting around and waiting. **No way.** Manifesting is so much more than that. It's creating a paradigm shift in your thinking and sending your mind down a new, more positive path.

We all have goals, dreams, and desires. There are so many things we want to see in our lives. But sometimes we think that we can't ever get there. There always seem to be so many obstacles that stand in our way. Look back to the affirmation chapter. So many of us can relate to the feeling of *we aren't good enough*, or *we'll never get there*, or *we can't achieve that*. Guess what?

You're just using the concept of manifestation but in reverse. We don't even realise how we've used manifestation when we're stuck in our negative swirling minds. We've pulled in all the bad things in our lives, and those are the only things we can see. Why not put the skill of manifestation to good use and set our minds toward positive goals and positive outcomes? It's a little bit harder, yet the rewards you will reap will be endless.

Manifestation is nothing new. Even though it's a hot topic now, the concept started coming around because of a book published in 1937, called *Think and Grow Rich* by Napoleon Hill. In his book, he stressed the idea, "You are the master of your destiny."

This concept was something very unique. Imagine it. We are not victims to the whims of fate or chance, or accident. We can step up, take charge, throw back our shoulders, and take steps towards the kind of lives we want. We are the **masters** of our own lives, our own futures, and our own destinies. How empowering is this?

Upleveling yourself and manifesting your *future you* is connected to the **Law of Attraction**. This law states that you can manifest what you want in your life by believing it.

You can bring positive things into your life through what you think about and decide. You may not believe it, but it's our brain that really makes our lives what we want them to be. All we need to do is set our brains down the right trail, and then we can achieve anything we want to do.

The future is in our hands. We are holding the power, yet we are too afraid to use it because it takes effort, time, and we just don't know what it will be like to achieve our goals. Success can be a scary thing, especially if you're not used to finding it or even accepting it when it comes.

Consider Maya Angelou's quote at the start of the chapter. Choose your wish, and then be prepared when you get it. That's similar to 'be careful what you wish for'. That's why manifestation should be handled and used correctly, just like affirmations.

The issue is that many people think that affirmations and the idea of manifestation is a lot of 'mumbo-jumbo'. They get the impression that all it is is writing something down or saying something to themselves every day, and that's all.

Not at all. It's actual work. The affirmation and the belief in your future is only the first step. You need to **take steps** to manifest the future that you desire. It's a little similar to prayer. You can't just ask for what you want and sit idly by, hoping that whatever power you've prayed to will bring your desires and lay them in your lap. You need to keep working towards your goal.

For example, while Jim Carrey was trying to create his comedy career, he wrote himself a cheque for ten million dollars. He kept that cheque with him as a symbol that he was going to have a great future. He was going to find the career that he wanted. Ten years later, he starred in *Dumb and Dumber*, and the rest is history.

While that sort of dramatic flair may not appeal to everyone, the concept is still understood. That is manifestation. You want to say to the universe, "Hey, I want so and so. I'm going to work for it, but I'm putting my energy out there to get so and so."

That is what the Law of Attraction states. The belief is that the world is full of energy, and we live lives based on the positive or negative energy that we put out into the universe. It is so easy to be full of negativity. The world is certainly full of it.

Like energy *attracts* like energy, so if you're focused on negativity, that is the energy you're going to attract into your life. That's the lens you're going to look through, and everything that happens to you will filter through that lens.

But if you put out positive energy and have your thoughts centred towards positive affirmations and positive goals, that will draw positive energy to you. Good things will come your way, according to the Law of Attraction.

What can you manifest? You can manifest anything that you desire. Most people are searching for more money, success in their careers, true love, self-improvement, and so much more. Instead of doubting that you'll ever get where you want to get, start believing.

There are a few tips to keep in mind:

- **Make your goals as clear and concise as you possibly can.** For example, what does success in your chosen career look like to you?

- **Be consistent.** Keep repeating this goal. Keep it in your mind; write it down; put it in a place you can see it, or make a vision board.

- **Take steps to achieve this goal.** Let's say you're looking to lose weight. Sitting around and doing nothing won't get you there. Take important steps to create achievements.

- **Be present and mindful.** Things may not come to you as quickly as you hoped, and sometimes, you might end up getting something better that you didn't even realise you needed! Be open to your goal changing and growing as you take steps toward it.

- **Cultivate gratitude.** This is what journaling is ALL about. Building a life of gratitude and an attitude of thankfulness will change everything about who you are. Remember to always be thankful for the things that come your way, even if they aren't exactly what you were looking for. Wake up happy, thankful, and ready to face the day ahead.

Now is the time to start manifesting your future self in order to uplevel your life. Often people think they will be happy 'when' they reach a goal, or 'when' they have hit a particular milestone. You need to start manifesting **now**. You need to start believing **now** for the dream to become a reality. Journaling is a fantastic way to begin this process. Your journal is a part of yourself where you can share anything. You can write down your fears, your hopes, and your dreams. It's a place to work out your frustrations as you begin to work towards the future you want.

But it can also be a place where you take practical steps to manifest exactly what you're looking for. Choose a goal and an affirmation. Where do you hope to be? What is it that you want to see in your future? Who would you like to be?

Write it down. And write it down again. Each day take the time to write down your affirmations in order to keep your mind in the vein of positive, effective thinking. Write down what it will look like when you achieve that goal. Be specific to visualise that future and keep it in mind as you go through each day.

Pick a time of day that's best for you and sit down with your manifestations. It could be five minutes, ten minutes, an hour. It doesn't matter. All that matters is that you are being reflective, visualising your future, and spending time to help make it happen. Guided journaling is your ticket to finding the future you have been looking for for so long.

Just one thing. Affirmations only work when you believe them. It bears repeating that you need to make your goals something that is both realistic and optimistic. While Jim Carrey's example is a great way to showcase the idea of manifesting, it may not be realistic for everyone.

Pick the goals that are a part of your reality. Things that you can achieve if you take steps to make them happen. For example, a fish can't one day hope to live on land. Find affirmations and goals that you can believe in and take with you as you face each day. Daily journaling will help you bolster this belief, strengthen it, and bring about its fruition.

It might all sound silly or pointless. There is the old and tired saying of 'just think positively'. That can be frustrating because that isn't really a helpful solution with steps to follow.

Let's say you're having a challenging time, and you're in a really negative headspace. You call a friend on the phone, and they tell you, 'it'll all work out, just think positively'. You may want to scream and slam the phone down in response because that doesn't actually help with anything.

Just think positive! Are you kidding me? That asks you to make an incredible shift of the mind instantly without putting any work into it. This is actually the reason why I created this method of journaling for myself. Whilst I believe you can attempt to think positively and hope for a better future, the reality is that we need to work for it. It's very easy to let our day-to-day lives take over, and we forget to manifest the future. We forget to be grateful. We forget to be positive. Small, simple strategies in your daily journaling can help us stay on top of everything and manifest the future of our dreams.

But if we boil that advice down, 'thinking positively' is essentially manifesting, just not specific. For example, pick something that you're hoping for, such as, "I will be a better listener to those who share with me."

The goal is hopeful and specific, and the statement is strong. Now, you can take that into your journal each day and brainstorm how that looks to you. Perhaps you specifically want to be a better listener to your kids, your partner, or your colleague. Each day, you can think about how that goal will look for you that day.

Each day keep practising manifesting what you want, in this case, better and more meaningful relationships. Using your journal will help you to create tangible plans that can set you in motion.

Don't stop there. Let's say you've achieved the goal you were hoping for. You manifested something positive into your life. There is so much more to be done. It might be easier to start small as you begin to understand the manifesting process as well as the journaling process. It can also bolster your courage and confidence in the process before you start reaching for the ultimate goal.

But whatever it is, know that you can achieve it. With the right tools, like a strong, specific affirmation, and a trusty journal in whatever shape or form, you can make almost anything happen. Attract like energy to yourself using the Law of Attraction. Even if you are doubtful, think of the alternative – living a life set in negativity that spirals into despair and hopelessness? Instead, choose a life in search of the things you want, focusing on gratitude and hope. **Manifest** the good.

Chapter Summary

To sum up...

- Manifesting is the act of sending out positive energy in order to receive positive energy back in the form of your desires.

- Ask for what you want. Create goals and affirmations that are clear and concise, things that are easy to remember and to visualise.

- Work hard and take steps to achieve this. Don't sit back and expect to be handed your better future. It takes effort to achieve goals, even with the help of the Law of Attraction.

- Journal your way to manifest what you want. Use daily journaling to help plan out and visualise what you hope to achieve. Build up your confidence and belief in the *future you.*

Congratulations, you did it! You've finished section one and now about to head into section two. In this next section, we will dive into the **nitty-gritty** of creating balance. You will begin with learning about how to start the guided journaling process for your **heart**.

PART TWO

Getting into the Nitty-Gritty

CHAPTER SIX

Focusing on the heart

"The best and most beautiful things cannot be seen or even touched. They must be felt with the heart." – **Helen Keller**

What makes your heart full? What makes it feel light, happy, and content? Perhaps it's meditation, spending time with family, listening to music, touching your bare feet to grass, a drink with a friend. Whatever it might be, now is the time to find the activities that fill your heart with happiness and make you feel whole and complete.

In this chapter, we will focus on the heart and how to create a lifestyle and mindset through journaling that helps your heart. We always like to think of the heart as an emotional entity whenever we discuss mental health. But mental and physical health are inextricably linked. So, you helping your emotional heart through daily guided journaling will also help your physical one.

It's been proven! A 2005 study states that those who write for about 15-20 minutes per day, 3-5 times a week will help reduce their blood pressure, lower cortisol, and limit stress-related illnesses, which result in less doctor visits! Those are all great things for your physical heart. Yet, how can journaling help your emotional heart, the heart that guides you through life by its feelings, both positive and negative?

Frequent journaling is like putting a little pause on your day-to-day life. Things can get hectic sometimes, and especially now, in today's frenzied world, we don't take enough time just to sit and be with ourselves. It can be a daunting thought to have to sit and be with our feelings and thoughts. Sometimes, so many get backed up in our minds and hearts that when we actually do sit down, it's like they suddenly all come bursting forth, making quiet time a little difficult and painful.

But with writing and journaling, you aren't just sitting and thinking. It's like an added layer to meditation. You're physically moving and writing down as the thoughts come to your mind. It's unbelievably therapeutic. Just like talking to a therapist, you can **unburden** your heart through journaling.

Journaling for your heart can also give you:

- peace of mind
- a feeling of immense gratitude
- lift your spirits and vibrational energy
- more organised, less frenzied thoughts

- an understanding of your emotions
- a chance to get to know yourself a little bit better
- reminders to participate in activities that fill your heart
- and the list goes on!

This may also be an excellent solution for those who are a little reticent about counselling or even sharing their emotions with others. With a journal, it's just between you and the page. There is no judgment, and you can write freely about anything that comes to your mind and heart. You can feel yourself releasing burdens as you write and gaining insight into your own heart.

So, what are some ways that you can journal for the heart? There is no one perfect way, but you do need to find a method that works for you, your emotions, and your schedule. Usually, people like to select a particular time of day that suits them and stick to that day. Choose a time where you can actually take at least ten minutes to be alone without interruption. Some may find they have time in the morning, but for others, the night-time is better when all is quiet. Or you might even think about working on it during a lunch break. I know many in the '5am club' that awake an hour before their families to meditate, stretch, and journal.

You can use your journal as a gratitude journal. Either list or write out the things that you are grateful for and make your heart happy each day. It's a great reminder to look out for the good things in your life instead of letting the bad weigh down on your heart. If you're writing at the end of the day, you can simply recount what happened during your day, focusing on something special that made you feel happy or grateful.

Or, you could write about your feelings as they come. This is a great choice for those morning writers. How are you feeling today? What emotion is the strongest at this moment? What emotion do I hope to feel by the end of the day? Or what emotion would be the best to keep me motivated and happy throughout the day?

Also, another excellent journaling solution is to combine it with meditation. If you find meditation useful and effective for your life, then putting it together with journaling will multiply the benefits tenfold! Spend time in meditation, however long you wish, and then take the time to write down what kinds of feelings and thoughts were going through your mind. They could either be negative or positive.

If negative, then journaling is the way to get them out of your mind onto a page (this is a very proactive way of stopping the cycle of negative thinking). If your feelings are positive, then you can write them down to remind yourself of them. You can always refer back to them when you feel as if your heart needs a little booster.

Start the Process

As the saying goes, 'proper preparation prevents poor performance'. It's often a saying used in sports or business goal-setting strategies, but the same is true for journaling. Creating a goal for your journaling habits can make a big difference. You can do this analysis once a year, every three months, or monthly; it's up to you, but it will make an impact on the effectiveness of your journaling.

Start with a little *check-in* with yourself. There is an accompanying downloadable ebook that you can use to begin this process.   Use the allocated pages to focus specifically on the heart. Focus on these four actions: *Reflect, Dream, Bridge the Gap, and Decide* to get you on your way and answer the questions under each of the actions.

- **REFLECT:** Where is your heart now? How do you feel emotionally? What is weighing down your heart, and what is making your heart full?

- **DREAM:** How do you want to feel? Where do you want to focus your emotions? What positive emotions do you want to encourage, and what negative emotions do you want to discourage? Make sure you consider long-term and short-term dreams. If you can dream it, you can do it. If it doesn't scare you a little, then you're probably not dreaming big enough.

- **BRIDGE THE GAP:** How can you bridge the gap between where you are now and where you want to be? What do you feel you lack in this area, and what would you like to improve upon? What activities, methods, or tools could help you achieve your 'dream you'? Some

HEART

REFLECT
Where are you now?

EXPRESS GRATITUDE
for what your heart gives you

DREAM
What do you really want?

EXPRESS GRATITUDE
for what the future brings

MANIFEST
how you really want to feel

BRIDGE THE GAP
What are you missing?

EXPRESS GRATITUDE
for what lies ahead

Create **AFFIRMATIONS**
to support your heart's desire

MANIFEST
what you want by making a decision

DECIDE
What are you going to do?

EXPRESS GRATITUDE
for what lies ahead

Create **AFFIRMATIONS**
to support your hearts' needs

JOURNALING AFFIRMATIONS

**YOGA
MEDITATION
SELF LOVE
EARTHING
READING
MUSIC**

HEART

EXPRESS GRATITUDE
for your heart

MANIFEST
your heart's desire

Create **AFFIRMATIONS**
to nourish your heart

examples are meditation, yoga, practising gratitude, writing 'I am' statements or affirmations, listening to music, motivational books, earthing, journaling (of course!).

- **DECIDE:** What time frame are you basing these goals on - one month, three months, one year? What activities, methods, or tools are you willing to commit during this time? What milestones do you want to reach? How will you reward yourself when you reach these goals? How will you use your journal to help you **commit** to and **achieve** these goals? It could be simply through daily affirmations that you will use to create belief in yourself or perhaps a ten-minute journaling session after you do your morning meditation. Whatever it is, use your **SMART goals** to make sure you decide on an action that is specific, measurable, achievable, realistic, and timely.

Use the Tools

Once you've made your decisions for matters of the heart, we can begin the process of journaling. Here is where we put into practice the affirmations, gratitude techniques, and manifesting tools, plus any other activities that support the heart. Now is when we start to use our journal to *Bridge the Gap* and support our *Decisions*.

No matter what you're hoping to achieve through your journal, in this case, a happy heart, you need affirmations! Using affirmations can help guide your journaling towards a specific goal. During the *Reflect, Dream, Bridge the Gap, and Decide* process is a great time to pick new affirmations, keep old ones, or make minor adjustments.

Affirmations need to be short and simple, easy to remember. They are positive, powerhouse statements that remind you of something you often forget or express a goal you're trying to achieve. For example, a woman's heart may be feeling heavy because she is a *highly sensitive person*. She's very attuned to the feelings of herself, others, and the energy in the world. It can be both a weakness and a strength.

However, this woman may be feeling run down because she grasps onto the negative energy of others and takes their comments to heart. She doesn't need to change herself and how she processes information that she receives from the world, but she does need to form a protective barrier to things that don't serve her. This is where affirmations can come in.

She could select an affirmation such as "I will release negative comments that no longer serve me." Her statement is strong, using the powerful intro words, 'I will'. It is not something she might do or will try to do. She **will** do it and **will** achieve it. As she writes in her journal, she can focus on this affirmation, maybe even writing it at the top of the page.

Then, the rest of her journaling time can be focused on that goal. What is she feeling now that she needs to release? What are some good things that she needs to hold on to? What will her day look like if she's focused on releasing negative energy that comes her way?

Next, it's very useful to put manifesting into practice. Manifesting is believing that you can achieve something. It's sending out positive energies into the world in order to attract that positivity into your life: the Law of Attraction.

So, if you have a goal that you're interested in, write it down, and then begin to take steps toward that goal.

Another valuable tool for manifestation is a vision board. Cut out images that inspire you to achieve this goal. What will your goal of releasing negative energy bring to you that you desire? Keep that vision board nearby as you spend time in your journal working through this manifestation. Journal about how achieving your goal will make you feel. Set tiny milestones along the way, so you can feel gratitude for making small changes as you go. There are so many ways to do this, and you can choose what works for you!

It may be starting to sound just a little bit complicated and overwhelming. But this is the exact reason we *Bridge the Gap and Decide*. Making a plan for your journaling directs you to *Decide* what's most important for you right now and allows you to create a simple strategy to reach this goal. Sit back, close your eyes, and take a moment to visualise your journaling and what your journaling space will look like. It's quiet, and either the sun is just beginning to rise above the horizon, or it's already dark outside. You can hear the sound of the birds or the breeze rustling the leaves. No one is talking to you; there are no demands on your time just yet. It's only you, with a pen in your hand and a journal before you. All you need to do at this moment is to think about **you!**

What does your heart want? What do you want out of this time with yourself? Close your eyes and think about what your heart is trying to say to you that it can't say when the world around you is full of chaos. Then, begin to write. Let it flow out of you easily and without reserve. As the poet William Wordsworth said,

*"Fill your paper with the
breathings of your heart."*

Doesn't sound so awful, does it? You may even find your heart feeling calm at the mere prospect of getting started. Build your heart back up and strengthen it, making it full—uplevel your life through journaling for the heart. Let your heart rest in the words of the page, unburden itself, and release all the negative things weighing it down. Not only will journaling help your emotional heart, but it could make a big difference for your physical heart as well!

***

*There is a free resource available to download to help you use this journaling method. It will give you a visual display of how to get started. There are also several guided journals available for purchase that encompass these principles and your particular choice of focus. For example, there is a guided journal specifically for focusing on **self-love** whilst maintaining life balance.*

You can find samples of all our journals at
turtlepublishing.com.au.

Chapter Summary

To sum up...

- Think about what makes your heart full. Focus on these activities when creating your journal.

- Journaling is proven to help your physical heart! It can reduce stress, blood pressure, and cortisol.

- *Reflect, Dream, Bridge the Gap, and Decide*: Regularly work through questions about the state of your heart and your goals for your heart that you want to achieve .

- Use affirmations to tether yourself to a goal and a vision for the future.

- Manifest what you want your future to be. Believe it. Create a vision board; write down steps to bring you closer to your goal; send out positive energy into the world.

- Visualise yourself journaling and your journaling space. What does it look like? How does it make you feel? How can you get started?

In the next chapter, you will learn about how to journal for overall **health**. While journaling for the heart can help your health in many ways, you can also journal for the whole body and make yourself feel brighter, more energised, and invigorated, ready to tackle whatever life brings your way.

CHAPTER SEVEN

Journaling for health

*"To keep the body in good health is a duty...
otherwise we shall not be able to keep the
mind strong and clear."* - **Buddha**

Typically, people think of journaling as a way to help boost your mental and emotional health, but it can also help you with your physical health. Besides, physical health is one of the most important ways to improve your mental health. However, it often gets forgotten or pushed aside when people get busy. People usually don't stop to take a look at their physical health unless something significant happens to them. They ignore the little signs along the way. The world is so busy and their lives so full that anything your body is trying to tell you gets drowned out in all the noise.

That's why journaling health goals is popular. It helps you re-establish that link to your physical body by planning, reflecting, and recording. Think of all the ways that we can improve our physical health: exercise, good sleep, enough water, good nutrition, sunshine, and so much more. Sometimes, the list of what people need to do to stay in good health can be a little daunting, but you can make it smooth, easy, and organised with journaling

You don't have to be working towards an extreme physical health goal to make it worthwhile. It can simply be a way to stay connected each day with how you feel so that you can listen to your body's signals about what it needs.

Journaling for health can give you so much, such as:

- A plan and a way to reflect on how you're feeling and what goals you have

- A sense of accomplishment in recording and seeing progress

- The motivation to keep going

- A way to understand how certain foods affect your energy and mood

- A way to analyse how it's making you feel and what's working/not working

Often, people put their physical health on the back burner. There's just too much going on, and people think that they'll just wait until there's a better time. There's a big project coming up at work. The kids have to go to practices or have a big show coming up. The grandparents are ailing, and things need to be decided about their future. Whatever it might be, there is something that you need to realise: **things will always come up.**

They won't end one day. Things are always going to fill your schedule, and that's not a bad thing. It shows that you have a full life. Perhaps you might need to take a few things out of it if it's getting too much, but it's not as if there's a magical day where there will be nothing going on. The time to start working on your physical health is **now.**

Just like with mental health, there will always be thoughts rushing in and out of your head, whether good or bad. It's all about how you control them and react to them that makes the most significant difference. It's the same with physical health: it's all about how you control your schedule and set aside time to reflect on it that will make the most significant difference.

My personal experience with journaling has allowed me to realise that health is my most important life aspect in maintaining life balance. It's my commitment to my health that allows me to juggle life the best. When I drop exercising, all the other balls drop! I lack focus for work, I have less patience with my children, I lose energy to prepare nutritious food, which then reduces my ability to exercise consistently. It's a vicious cycle. It was through journaling that I realised this pattern and why I'm so passionate about helping others discover their triggers through journaling.

You can start small. It can be as simple as at the end of each day recording how your body feels. Do you have a headache or a stomachache? Maybe you feel a little too tired or even weak? Record this down in your journal and see if you can spot any patterns in how you feel, and find any links. See if you begin to think about and assess how you feel during the day, even without a journal. For example, you might have a banging headache during the day, and in checking out your past entries, you noticed that you also had a headache when you didn't drink enough water.

You drink more water, and then you start to feel better. This is precisely the kind of thing that journaling for your health can do for you, even if it seems small. Then, as time goes on, you can start to do bigger things with your journal to help maintain your physical health.

Here are some great tips for how to create a journal focused on your health:

- Create a reflection section that describes how you feel about your body and what kinds of things you're experiencing: maybe interrupted sleep, sugar cravings, etc.

- Write down a few goals you have that you can see yourself achieving in the near future: maybe you want to lose five kilograms, drink more water, or get eight hours of sleep.

- Plan out your exercise for the week, and afterwards, record how it felt. This is a great place to write down what worked or what didn't (especially what kinds of exercise you enjoyed and what you didn't).

- Schedule an activity that fulfils more than one part of your life at once - for example, a walk with your family (health and relationships) or yoga with a friend (health, relationships, and heart)

- Plan out time for rest during the week and what that rest will look like. Sometimes people won't take rest or exercise until it's built into their schedule. And rest is just as important as exercise!

Start the Process

Just like the last chapter, let's use the structure to *check-in* with yourself to get started on your health journal. Go through the actions of *Reflect, Dream, Bridge the Gap, and Decide*. Remember, you will find a download for these practices at the beginning of this book. This can be done at the beginning of the month, every three months, or more often. It's totally up to you!

- **REFLECT:** According to you, where is your health now? How is your weight, sleep, nutrient/water intake, etc.? How do you feel day-to-day? What are your energy levels like?

- **DREAM:** How do you want to feel? How would you like to look? What kind of health changes would you like to make? Are there any health challenges you have that you would like to overcome or eliminate from your life? Are there any new physical accomplishments you'd like to reach - like running a marathon, for example? Make sure you consider long-term and short-term dreams. If you can dream it, you can do it. If it doesn't scare you a little, then you're probably not dreaming big enough.

- **BRIDGE THE GAP:** How can you bridge the gap between where you are now and where you want to be? What do you feel you lack in this area, and what would you like to improve upon? What activities, methods, or

HEALTH

REFLECT
Where are you now?

DREAM
What do you really want?

BRIDGE THE **GAP**
What are you missing?

DECIDE
What are you going to do?

EXPRESS GRATITUDE
For what your health gives you

EXPRESS GRATITUDE
for what the future brings

MANIFEST
the physical & mental health that you desire

EXPRESS GRATITUDE
for what lies ahead

Create **AFFIRMATIONS**
to support your health goals

EXPRESS GRATITUDE
for what lies ahead

Create **AFFIRMATIONS**
to help reach your health goals

MANIFEST
what you want by making a decision

JOURNALING AFFIRMATIONS

EXERCISE
NUTRITION
WATER
SLEEP PATTERNS
BREATHING
REST & RECOVERY

HEALTH

EXPRESS GRATITUDE
for your health

MANIFEST
your ultimate health goals

Create **AFFIRMATIONS**
for that strengthen your health goals

tools could help you achieve your 'dream you'? Some examples are setting certain exercise routines, planning or preparing a nutrition guide, setting sleep routines, breathing exercises, allocating time in the sunshine.

- **DECIDE:** What time frame are you basing these goals on - one month, three months, one year? What activities, methods, or tools are you willing to commit during this time? What milestones do you want to reach? How will you reward yourself when you reach these goals? How will you use your journal to help you **commit** to and **achieve** these goals? It could be simply a daily reminder to drink your water or write an affirmation about feeling full of energy. Whatever your choice, use your **SMART goals** to make sure you decide on an action that is specific, measurable, achievable, realistic and timely.

During this reflection time, you can set the path for the rest of the month. Instead of just vaguely knowing in which direction you want to go and hoping it works, journaling can now assist you in obtaining a vision of achieving your goals.

That's why it's important to do this *check-in* regularly. You can Reflect on how things have been progressing thus far and remind yourself of how to keep implementing your health goals in the future.

Use the Tools

Think of health as your reason to journal, with affirmations and manifesting as the most powerful tool in your kit. Set one or more affirmations for yourself each month or at least throughout the life of your goal. Not only does your health plan keep you on track, but so does your affirmation. It reminds you of your overarching goal.

For example, let's say that you've been struggling to get enough sleep each night. You haven't made it a priority in the last few years, and the consequences have been showing in your life and your work. Make an affirmation such as, "I will make sleep a priority, and will stop working or watching TV at least one hour before it's time for bed."

The affirmation is strong, clear, and specific (which is what an affirmation needs to be in order to be effective!) You know what you're meant to do. It gives you an easy picture of what your work toward achieving your goal of more sleep will look like. Write this down in your journal in your physical health section. It may even be something you want to write down every day or post up somewhere in your house to remind you that you want sleep to be a priority.

Under your affirmation, you can write down some ways to fight against temptations or deal with awkward situations when it comes to being unable to fulfil your goal. Also, record your successes. How do you feel after you've achieved your goal? Is it an attainable goal? Do you feel motivated to continue?

You must also use manifesting in your health journal. Believe that you can achieve the goals that you have set for yourself. Using the Law of Attraction, your positive thinking and belief can help bring positive energy to your life, thus helping you succeed with your goals. A vision board is a great way to help encourage you in your physical health goals. It's especially effective for this aspect of life change!

Simply writing in your journal to remind yourself to look at your vision board can make an incredible difference in how you feel about your goals and the energy you bring to them.

This year, this month, this moment, make your physical health a priority and use journaling to uplevel it. Journaling for your health can mean the difference between staying where you are at and your current health struggles, to achieve things you've wanted to do for so long. If you have a range of physical health goals and hopes, then take it one step at a time. It can be unbelievably daunting to try to tackle everything at once, and that's a big reason why people often don't even get started.

But you have the tools now to begin. You know how you can structure your journal, but now you have to think about exactly what you want to get out of it. If you're struggling to figure out which aspect of physical health you want to focus on, then it's time for the reflection we discussed earlier. Sit down and take a little time to think about your body, how it's feeling, and what changes or improvements you might want to make in your health and lifestyle. Choose what you think is the most important right then.

For example, finding time to rest in your life may take a higher priority than attempting your first marathon. Pick your goal; create an affirmation; complete your *Reflect, Dream, Bridge the Gap, and Decide* process, and then you're off! You're ready to use journaling to make a big difference in your physical health. And remember, the mind and body are linked. One affects the other significantly. Both the act of journaling and what you're journaling about will help you make changes in both your mental and physical health.

***

*There is a free resource available to download to help you use this journaling method. It will give you a visual display of how to get started. There are also some specific pages in this download that will help you record your daily health habits. There are also several guided journals available for purchase that encompass these principles and your particular choice of focus. For example, there is a guided journal specifically for focusing on **health** whilst maintaining life balance.*

You can find samples of all our journals at
turtlepublishing.com.au.

Chapter Summary

To sum up...

- Journaling is not just for mental health; you can also use it for physical health.

- Physical and mental health are inextricably linked, and if you work on one, it will help the other!

- Journaling for your health can give you a plan of how to move forward, a place to reflect on the past, and the motivation to keep going!

- Use *Reflect, Dream, Bridge the Gap, and Decide* to get started on your health journal.

- Use your journal to create nutrition plans, exercise plans, rest and sleep schedules, and more!

- If it seems too daunting, start small. Pick one goal and one affirmation and go from there!

In the next chapter, you will learn how you can use journaling to create good habits that **feed the mind**. You've learned how to journal for the heart and overall health; now it's time to work on that big, beautiful brain.

CHAPTER EIGHT

Habits to feed your mind

"Stock your mind. It is your house of treasure and no one in the world can interfere with it."
– Frank McCourt

The mind: it can play tricks on you or be a wonderful ally. It has so much power, so much capability, yet many of us don't nurture it, and we let outside forces control it.

As John Milton said,

"the mind is its own place, and in itself, can make a Heaven of Hell, or a Hell of Heaven."

These are telling words because they are oh, so true. The mind is our epicentre. While the physical body controls our movements and affects how we feel, it is our mind that holds our dreams, our futures, our powers in its grasp. And we need to do the work to keep our minds active, healthy, and nourished. We can make a 'Heaven out of Hell' in our own minds. We can choose to look on the brighter side. Nourishing our minds with personal development can help us do this more consistently. Let's look at what we already know about things that can help 'feed the mind'.

- Lectures, such as Ted Talks, or even course lectures
- Academic courses that you can do online or in-person
- Listening to informative, interesting podcasts
- Listening to interviews of inspiring individuals
- Reading, especially books that provide you new knowledge and new insights

These are just a few of the ways, as adults, we can work to improve our minds. The education and nourishing of our minds can continue after high school or college. We can keep it going in small ways that could make a huge difference.

One of the big questions that could be asked is why? *Why keep learning after formal schooling is finished.* Some people might consider that it is a waste of time as there is already so much to do. They are already doing so much at work or home and don't have time to sit and work on a 'useless' topic, such as learning a new language or taking a drawing course.

Well, guess what? You are reading this book, looking for a secret to a better life and a better future. This is it. You are **already** up-levelling yourself by finding habits that feed your mind. Studies show that continued learning can lead to a happier and a longer life. There are also studies that link continued learning with a variety of benefits from delaying the symptoms of Alzheimer's to making more money. It is often heard, learners are earners. Whatever way you look at it, keeping your mind nourished is only positive.

And it's fun. You can find something that really interests you. Remember the joy of learning that you felt as a child? Remember when you first found something that got you really excited, and you wanted to keep reading everything there was about it? Maybe it was dinosaurs, or mystery novels, or even plants and gardening. Continued learning doesn't mean you need to sit around and listen to someone talk about something you hate.

It's about choosing to gain more knowledge in ways that both serve you and interest you. It's also a way to show love to yourself. You are giving your mind the food it needs to stay healthy and strong. And just like journaling can help keep your heart and body healthy, it can do the same for your mind.

Here's how:

- It can give you a safe place to write out your intentions. How do you want to nourish your mind? What are you interested in learning more about? What kinds of goals are you hoping to achieve in the area of your mind?

- It can also help you plan out how you will achieve your goals. Perhaps you can schedule a time to listen to a lecture or a podcast. Maybe you can think about starting a book club and write down the things you learn each month or each week.

MIND

REFLECT
Where are you now?

DREAM
What do you really want?

BRIDGE THE GAP
What are you missing?

DECIDE
What are you going to do?

EXPRESS GRATITUDE
For what you have now

EXPRESS GRATITUDE
For what the future brings

MANIFEST
what you really want

EXPRESS GRATITUDE
For the process of change

Create **AFFIRMATIONS**
to support your dreams

EXPRESS GRATITUDE
and **MANIFEST**
the future

Create **AFFIRMATIONS**
to support your progress

MANIFEST
what you want by making a decision

JOURNALING AFFIRMATIONS

**READING
COURSES
AUDIO BOOKS
EDUCATION
TED TALKS
PODCASTS**

MIND

EXPRESS GRATITUDE
for your mind

MANIFEST
opportunities for growth

Create **AFFIRMATIONS**
to support growth

- It could even be a safe space where you can write down all the new and interesting things you've learned from whatever activity you're doing. Perhaps you've been following a series on Ted Talks, and you want to take notes to refer to later.

Start the Process

Let's begin with the *Reflect, Dream, Bridge the Gap, and Decide* process. Just like in the other chapters, you need to do a little *check-in* with yourself before you can delve into useful, effective journaling to feed your mind.

- **REFLECT:** Where is your mind now? How do you feel about what you know? Have there been certain circumstances where you've felt like you lacked knowledge? Are you happy with the way in which you approach life? What do you wish you could change about your thoughts?

- **DREAM:** What would you like to learn? Are there specific personal development books or courses you'd like to complete? What knowledge could assist you with your dreams and aspirations? Make sure you consider long-term and short-term dreams. If you can dream it, you can do it. If it doesn't scare you a little, then you're probably not dreaming big enough.

- **BRIDGE THE GAP:** How can you bridge the gap between where you are now and where you want to be? What do you feel you lack in this area, and what would you like to improve upon? What activities, methods, or tools could help you achieve your 'dream you'? Some examples are lectures, audiobooks, reading, following inspiring role models, academic courses.

- **DECIDE:** What time frame are you basing these goals on - one month, three months, one year? What activities, methods, or tools are you willing to commit during this time? What milestones do you want to reach? How will you reward yourself when you reach these goals? How will you use your journal to help you **commit** to and **achieve** these goals? It could be simply scheduling a time to listen to your audiobook during your workout or researching online courses to improve your mindset. Whatever your choice, use your **SMART goals** to make sure you decide on an action that is specific, measurable, achievable, realistic, and timely.

Use the Tools

Once you've checked in and decided on a course of action, you can get started. Perhaps you want to start small to give yourself a little practice at feeding your mind before moving onto the bigger things. For example, maybe you want to spend more time improving your positive thoughts. Your goal could be to listen to an audiobook each morning or each night and then write down a little reflection of what you've learned. It's easy; it's clear, and you have an achievable and quantifiable goal.

Another way to make your path smoother is to use your affirmations and the tool of manifesting to get you where you want to go. These statements are a way to keep you grounded as you move along in your progress. Maybe you get distracted by getting busy, or you start to lose confidence that you can achieve your goals. But if you write down your affirmations in your journal and keep them in your head, they can help you stay on the path towards getting what you want. Like the earlier statement about listening, your affirmation can be something small and specific. That will make it a lot easier to use and to achieve.

Let's say you are a small business owner. You have built this business on your own, but you're looking to keep improving and expanding. Maybe you want to keep learning more about business to make it even better. Your affirmation could be something like: I will become a better businessperson. I will learn one new marketing strategy each day/week/month and put it into practice.

That affirmation is strong, confident, and it's to the point. You know precisely what you have to do to get started and to keep going. But remember to figure out where exactly you want to get your marketing strategies. Use your journal to write them down and then record ways you can implement the strategy or reflect on how they worked in your own business. It's as simple as that.

Another skill to master is the art of manifesting. It's been buzzing around social media these days because people are finding a lot of success in actually **believing** that they can achieve what they desire. Manifesting is sending out positive vibrational energies into the world to bring positive vibrations to oneself. It's believing, not getting bogged down with the fears and negative mindsets that often come when one is trying to work towards a goal.

But it's also about doing things to bring positivity to you. It's a lot more than just positive thinking and wishing and hoping for the best. That's where your journal comes in. It's the place where you can write down ways to take steps towards your goal. If you want to improve your writing, for example, then think about signing up for a beginner's writing course. It wouldn't make sense just to hope you'll get better at writing, and then that's all you do. Manifest your future by working towards it and playing a positive part in the universe.

What a lot of people don't realise is that we are in fact holding ourselves back. We see others achieving far more than us, and we often think, *I could never do that*, or perhaps, *they must be smarter than me* and so on. In reality, it's about us believing in what we can achieve. It's about taking steps towards those things. It can be difficult; it can be really hard, because using affirmations and manifesting, and even journaling takes us out of ourselves. We have to put the effort in to get something out.

Something a lot of people want is to feel confident when speaking in groups. They want to be able to have something interesting to share with others. They want an opportunity to teach another something that they care about. Consider a woman who has always felt lacking in confidence when it comes to reading, for example. Perhaps she doesn't feel very well-read, and she feels totally out of place in discussions when people talk about books.

She wants to change that. It means a lot to her that she can participate in such discussions and feel like she's contributing. She also wants to work on it for her own sake and think about something other than family or her career. So, she joins a book club. She starts reading books she would never have read before, and now she's kept accountable because her book club members depend on her. She goes to structured meetings where they discuss what they've learned, and if she's been journaling along the way, she can participate effectively.

Just like that, she's up-levelled herself. She's started to achieve her goal of reading more. She's gained confidence in speaking in groups about books. She's learned more by reading more, and she has practised the process of reflecting and analysing what she's read, giving her mind amazing 'food.' What a beautiful gift she has given to herself.

And while you're learning new things, whether it's about your chosen career or it's simply a new topic that you're interested in, you'll naturally grow in strength and confidence as you go along. As the saying goes, *knowledge is power*. No knowledge is useless, and it gives you a gift each time you learn something new. You are feeding your mind, making it stronger, happier, and better equipped for whatever you want to do with your life.

***

There is a free resource available to download to help you use this journaling method. It will give you a visual display of how to get started. There are also several guided journals available for purchase that encompass these principles.

You can find samples of all our journals at
turtlepublishing.com.au.

Chapter Summary

To sum up...

- The mind is what you make it, and it needs nourishment.

- Think of habits you can create that feed your mind. Maybe it's listening to podcasts, reading self-help books, taking a course. Build your brain to keep your mind healthy and strong.

- Journaling can help you achieve your mind goals. Use it to plan, reflect, and schedule.

- Use the *Reflect, Dream, Bridge the Gap, and Decide* process to help create better mind-feeding habits.

- Use affirmations and manifesting to push you along as you work towards your mind goals. Don't forget. It takes work to get where you want to be.

- Keeping your mind healthy, happy, and strong will make a world of difference even if you can't see it right away.

In the next chapter, you will learn how to use your journal to work on your **relationships**. Relationships are so important, but just like so many things, they often fall by the wayside in our quest to achieve our own personal goals.

CHAPTER NINE

Working on relationships

"The good life is built with good relationships." – **Robert J. Waldinger**

What makes life worth living? What makes people want to keep going forward, keep working hard, and keep hoping for the best? **Relationships.** Companionship is something that we as humans absolutely need. That's why depression is so often linked to a lack of positive or healthy relationships. We need other people. It's proven.

However, the sad thing is that we may have relationships ranging from friendships to family members, spouses, and more, but we don't always give them the attention they need because other things get in the way. Maybe we're totally focused on work, that we don't give our families and friends enough of our time at the end of the day.

Perhaps we're so busy and focused on our families that we forget to call our parents or spend time with our friends. It could be that we're even too focused on ourselves and working so hard to make changes in our personal lives that our intimate relationships get overlooked.

There are so many obstacles that can easily slip in between relationships, causing distance and problems. It's up to you to make the changes needed in order to have healthy, effective, positive relationships that make our lives just that much fuller. Women especially can find themselves struggling in these kinds of situations because women are expected to 'have it all.' They have to be both career-driven and family-driven, and as they attempt to make everyone else around them happy, it can leave them feeling drained, spent, and their relationships less than happy.

Consider all the relationships in your life, especially the ones that mean the most to you. These can be:

- Romantic relationships
- Immediate family
- Extended family
- Friends
- Colleagues

Just giving a glance over the relationships you have in your life, what kinds of activities would you think would be the most helpful for keeping these relationships strong and healthy?

Think:

- Partner time: quiet dinners, movie nights, child-free conversations
- Phone calls: especially if this person lives far away
- Friend time: girls' nights out, friend game nights
- Family time: visiting an elderly relative, spending time with your kids, holidays

These are just a few examples of how one can improve relationships, and all of them centre around the concept of **time**. It's a fact: we all have limited time on earth, and so one of the greatest gifts you can give someone else is your time. And not the scraps of time that you can find here and there when you've done everything else you've needed to do, but real **quality** time. That's the way to make progress in relationships. It's the same way with yourself. When you get too busy to take time to give to yourself, everything else in your life suffers.

We live lives of delicate balance. Spend too much time on one thing; another thing suffers. When this comes to relationships, you are not the only one affected by letting them suffer. Those who love you and care for you also have to receive the consequences. It can be so easy to be imbalanced and constantly slip into states of imbalance, but we can use journaling to get ourselves back on the right path with our relationships.

By its very nature, journaling is a meditative way to focus the mind and take time to pause and reflect. That can be **incredible** for your relationships. A common excuse for

RELATIONSHIPS

REFLECT
Where are you now?

EXPRESS GRATITUDE
For what you have now

DREAM
What do you really want?

EXPRESS GRATITUDE
For what the future brings

MANIFEST
what you really want

BRIDGE THE GAP
What are you missing?

EXPRESS GRATITUDE
For the process of change

Create **AFFIRMATIONS**
to support your dreams

DECIDE
What are you going to do?

EXPRESS GRATITUDE and **MANIFEST** the future

Create **AFFIRMATIONS**
to support your progress

MANIFEST
what you want by making a decision

JOURNALING AFFIRMATIONS

HOLIDAYS
BBQS
DATE NIGHT
PHONE CALLS
FAMILY NIGHTS
GIRLS NIGHTS

RELATIONSHIPS

EXPRESS GRATITUDE
for relationships

MANIFEST
your ideal relationships

Create **AFFIRMATIONS**
to nourish & grow your relationships

suffering relationships is because there just doesn't seem to be enough time in the day! But taking a pause out of the day to sit and actually think about your relationships will help you be intentional about them. Because that's what makes life so much fun. Our relationships help make our lives exciting, interesting, and satisfying, so why should we put them on the back burner!

Use your journal to be intentional about your relationships, whether you have old ones that you need to fix or current ones that need maintenance. A journal is your place to write about your relationships and figure things out that need solving. You could write out ideas for how to spend time with your partner that would make both of you feel happy and fulfilled. You could reflect on how your current relationships are going. You could write out letters that you never send to people who have hurt you or you've hurt in the past to try to resolve some of those old feelings. You can use it to write about finding peace in those relationships that cannot be resolved.

It doesn't matter how you want to use your journal, but simply the act of taking the time to write about relationships is a significant first step to improving, repairing and maintaining them.

Start the Process

Just like in the other chapters, when we've discussed journaling for the heart, the body, and the mind, you need to do a little *check-in* with yourself before you can delve into useful, effective journaling to uplevel your relationships.

Use these now-familiar steps to start journaling for your relationships off right:

- **REFLECT:** How are you feeling about your current relationships? Consider all types of relationships as mentioned in the list above. Are there any particular ones that you think need a little work? Do you need to resolve some conflicts? Where are your relationships currently ranking in your life? Are there any relationships you're holding on to that aren't serving you any longer?

- **DREAM:** What kind of person do you want to be in all your relationships? What do you hope to achieve in your relationships? How much time would you love to devote to your relationships? What activities would you like to do to strengthen relationships or resolve conflicts? Make sure you consider long-term and short-term dreams. If you can dream it, you can do it. If it doesn't scare you a little, then you're probably not dreaming big enough.

- **BRIDGE THE GAP:** How can you bridge the gap between where you are now and where you want to be? What do you feel you lack in this area, and what would you like to improve upon? What activities, methods, or tools could help you achieve your 'dream you'? Some examples are partner dates, phone calls, friends' nights, visiting elderly relatives, family holidays.

- **DECIDE:** What time frame are you basing these goals on - one month, three months, one year? What activities, methods, or tools are you willing to commit during this time? What milestones do you want to reach? How will you reward yourself when you reach these goals? How will you use your journal to help you

commit to and **achieve** these goals? It could perhaps be writing a letter to someone who has hurt you (you don't have to send it) or committing time to a self-help book on improving your relationship with your partner. Whatever your choice, use your **SMART goals** to make sure you decide on an action that is specific, measurable, achievable, realistic, and timely.

Since relationships can be so varied and complex, this *Reflect, Dream, Bridge the Gap, and Decide* activity can be especially daunting. But just take a deep breath. Write down your answers, reflect, and then pick a course of action. The best idea is to start with something small or start with one particular relationship that you think really needs your attention and now. That will help make this whole thing just a little bit easier to swallow.

Use the Tools

A great way to get started is to add your affirmations and manifesting ideas into your journal. Pick an affirmation that is short, sweet, and to the point. As you reflect, there will be something that sticks out, something you want to work toward that will rise to the surface as the most important to you right now. For example, you might write, "I will spend more quality time with my partner."

This affirmation is clear and strong. The particular relationship is mentioned, but adding a little more specificity could make it even stronger. Quality time can be so vague. Think about how much time you could visualise yourself spending with your partner weekly. Perhaps you could edit it to say, "I will spend quality time with my partner two nights per week."

Perfect. Now, the affirmation is clear, concise, and very specific. Underneath your affirmation in your journal, you can write out which nights would work for you both each week and which activities you might like to do that fit under quality time.

Your affirmation about relationships could also be focused on your skills as part of the relationship. Maybe you are struggling in your marriage or romantic relationship because you don't like to share what's inside of you. You prefer silence to arguing or to sharing your most intimate feelings. This can be like cancer in a close relationship such as a marriage.

It could be something you're looking to work on, so you build your affirmation around that. For example, your affirmation could be, "I will communicate my thoughts and feelings to my partner during an argument." You have a specific, set, clear way to go about your relationship. The next time an argument comes, don't rush away, hiding your feelings, find a way to speak out. This is where the journaling comes in. That is the space to write down your fears or your ideas about how that communication will go.

It can even be a spot to reflect on how it went if you tried it and weren't sure it was as effective as you wanted it to be. Either way, an affirmation is there to support you and to guide you. It keeps you going when you feel like you don't know how to continue or you don't want to continue. The words 'I will' are two powerful little words. They can make the difference between staying as you are and building a better *future you*.

Manifesting is another excellent way to work on relationships. According to the idea of manifesting and the Law of Attraction, positive energy brings in positive actions and consequences, and the opposite is also true. It's unbelievably easy to get stuck in a negative cycle with thoughts such as, *we can never find our way out of this*, or *my children hate me*, or *I can't fix whatever is broken*.

Negative energy can suck the life out of us, but it's easy. Positive energy can bring us a whole new future, but it definitely takes work, and you can manifest a *future you* that has improved relationships through this mindset. You are armed with your affirmation and perhaps even a vision board about your relationship goals, but now it's time to take steps towards what you want.

Spend time writing in your journal about positive outcomes you want to see. When you begin to try things in your relationships, such as communicating your feelings, write down the good things that happened. Remember **gratitude** in your writing. Think about what makes you grateful for the relationships you have in your life. Instead of going into your relationships each day tied down with that negative baggage, start looking for the good. Start building your pathway towards a better future.

Often, this can happen in a marriage, for example, because there is so much history and possibly pain. But if both parties are happy to keep in the marriage, then that's a good start. And when you start looking for the good things or things to be grateful for, your mind will make a shift. It's no joke. Your brain will actually build new neural pathways because you're thinking in a different vein, not sticking to the old pathway that was taking you nowhere.

Maybe that means you start complimenting your spouse, sending a note of encouragement to a friend, or reminding your children just how much you love them. You might be surprised at what changes you will see after even a short time. That is manifesting. It takes work, but it is a powerful tool. It could be the secret to a happier you with healthier and stronger relationships.

***

There is a free resource available to download to help you use this journaling method. It will give you a visual display of how to get started. There are also several guided journals available for purchase that encompass these principles.

You can find samples of all our journals at
turtlepublishing.com.au.

Chapter Summary

To sum up...

- Relationships are what make life worthwhile, whether it's friends, family, or coworkers.

- So many obstacles can get in the way of having healthy relationships. We are either pulled too thin, or we give too much time to one, and another suffers.

- Journaling can help you achieve your relationship goals. It's all about being intentional: taking time out of the day and making plans on how to build or maintain effective relationships.

- Use the *Reflect, Dream, Bridge the Gap, and Decide* process to help *check-in* with yourself and create steps towards your relationship goals.

- Use affirmations and manifesting to push you along as you work towards your relationship goals. Building positive energy back into your relationships will do wonders!

- Don't forget to be grateful and make an effort to look for gratitude within your relationships.

In the next chapter, you will learn about journaling for building your **life mission**. This could be about your career, your vocation, or just the contribution that you hope to make to the world. Journaling can help you do all that, and you can find yourself more connected to the world and yourself than ever before.

CHAPTER TEN

Build your life mission

"Make your life a mission – not an intermission."
– Arnold H. Glasow

Whether you're religious or not, everyone understands the concept of having a purpose. We want a reason to get out of bed in the morning. There has to be more to life than simply slogging through, right? We, as humans, need purpose in our lives to keep going. Not only that, but it makes our lives brighter, sharper, and more worthwhile. Our purpose makes us feel like our time on earth was meaningful and will leave something behind us when we're gone.

We want to feel like we've used it to the best of our abilities. We know we don't have unending amounts of time to spare, so we make each moment we have meaningful. An article in Scientific American describes it like this:

"To feel meaningful is to feel immortal."

What a beautiful idea. Your purpose can change over time, but it's important to start thinking about what your purpose or life mission is or what you would like it to be. You can begin to build it through your journal, and it can provide you with more fulfilment than you expected. This life mission can be many things, whether related to your career or a contribution to the world. Remember, your mission or purpose is different from the personal areas of your life.

It's not the same as the goal, "I will be a better friend." It has a more significant scope than that. Think about what sort of legacy you want to give to the world. In what way can you make your life more meaningful? It can be a little vague, such as "I want to give of myself and my time to... (whatever cause). Or perhaps it could be more specific: "In my career, I want to help young girls discover their purpose by... (whatever it might be). It's up to you. And your journal can help to either figure it out or focus your efforts towards the life purpose you have decided upon.

This can feel just a tad bit overwhelming. It's not as if your life isn't already full of schedules, events, relationships, and personal goals; *I also need to think of a life mission?* **Just take a breath and relax.** The exercise of building a life mission is not meant to stress you out. It's about finding a purpose that fulfils you. It's about finding little ways to make your life even more meaningful and even more worthwhile. Even small things make a difference. Be encouraged by these words by Napoleon Hill:

*"If you cannot do great things, do
small things in a great way."*

You can use your journal as a daily escape to work towards this mission. Set an intention to spend time on this daily. Even journaling through other aspects of your life can help you figure out what you would like your mission to be. Through journaling, you can find out what you truly value and what lies at the heart of all that you do. That is a beautiful way to figure out what you would like your purpose to be. It may even come as a surprise to you when you look back through your writing.

Take a look at a few tips on how to use your journal to figure out your life mission:

- Write about your values. What means a lot to you in life? What topic really lights you up when you are in a conversation? What types of activities will you prioritise before most others. Perhaps it's women's issues, families, financial strength, independence, motherhood, etc.

- Create a list of people who could help you figure out what you want, and then speak to them.

- Create your list of 100 things you want to do in your life. You may begin to see a recurring theme of what you find important.

- Write your life as if it's already happening. This can be a great 'visual' for you. Spend time describing what an ideal day would look like, or precisely what you would be doing if you were living your purpose. Think about meaning and fulfilment.

MISSION

REFLECT
Where are you now?

EXPRESS GRATITUDE
For what you have now

DREAM
What do you really want?

EXPRESS GRATITUDE
For what the future brings

MANIFEST
what you really want

BRIDGE THE GAP
What are you missing?

EXPRESS GRATITUDE
For the process of change

Create **AFFIRMATIONS**
to support your dreams

EXPRESS GRATITUDE
and **MANIFEST**
the future

Create **AFFIRMATIONS**
to support your progress

MANIFEST
what you want by making a decision

DECIDE
What are you going to do?

JOURNALING AFFIRMATIONS

PLANNNG LEARNING MANIFESTING VISION BOARD GOAL SETTING CONTRIBUTION

MISSION

EXPRESS GRATITUDE
for your purpose

MANIFEST
your ultimate life mission

Create **AFFIRMATIONS**
to support your purpose

- Answer this question, "If money wasn't an issue, what would I do with my time?"

There are so many different ways to go about this, but we're breaking them down for you, so you can find the best angle to get started. And if you don't want to start so officially with lists and plans, then just spend some time each day in reflection. Once we give our minds the chance to settle and be quiet, we can dig deep and find out what gives meaning to our lives. We can discover what we value. Sometimes that can be a long journey, for often, our busy lives can get in the way of connecting with ourselves and what we really care about.

Start the Process

Just like when working through the other aspects of our lives, we can begin the journal with a *check-in* process. You guessed it: *Reflect, Dream, Bridge the Gap, and Decide* is the way to go before you begin creating a life mission through your journaling.

- **REFLECT:** Even before you do anything else, dig deep. What do you care about? What values do you hold? What topics light you up? Are you happy with your contribution to society? Does your current financial position reflect your future goals?

- **DREAM:** What are your wildest dreams? What mark do you want to leave upon the world? Who do you want to help? What do you want to achieve in your career? Make sure you consider long-term and short-term dreams. If you can dream it, you can do it. If it doesn't scare you a little, then you're probably not dreaming big enough.

- **BRIDGE THE GAP:** How can you bridge the gap between where you are now and where you want to be? What do you feel you lack in this area, and what would you like to improve upon? What activities, methods, or tools could help you achieve your 'dream you'? Some examples are vision boards, setting and reviewing goals, creating contribution projects, starting your own business, developing skills to uplevel in your work or business goals, and creating time for manifesting.

- **DECIDE:** What time frame are you basing these goals on - one month, three months, one year? What activities, methods, or tools are you willing to commit during this time? What milestones do you want to reach? How will you reward yourself when you reach these goals? How will you use your journal to help you **commit** to and **achieve** these goals? It could be as simple as creating an affirmation to use daily, 'I will succeed in my life purpose,' or perhaps planning the initial steps for launching a charity. Whatever your choice, use your **SMART goals** to make sure you decide on an action that is specific, measurable, achievable, realistic, and timely.

These are just some starter questions for you to get the ball rolling. It may also be helpful to read some articles, books, and studies about purpose to get your mind in the right place. When speaking of missions and purpose, it can be a bit vague and amorphous, so learning more about the purpose of life purpose and the beauty of meaning can go a long way to getting you where you want to be with your own purpose.

Use the Tools

Now, affirmations can be just as useful here as they are with the other aspects of your journaling. Once you've gone through your *check-in* process, start to boil down your mission goals with one or more affirmations. For example, if you're still in the searching process, your affirmation could be, "I will spend ten minutes each day journaling about my purpose and building my life mission." The affirmation is clear, powerful, and specific.

Let's say you already know where you'd like to start going. Your affirmation might be something like, "I will use my ability as a lawyer to provide pro-bono work for women in need." Again, it's specific and clear. But it can also look however you want it to look. Spend time using your journal to reflect and plan your next steps with your affirmations as the focal point.

Next is where manifesting comes in. This can especially be a very powerful tool in this aspect of your life. Manifest the future that you want to have. Perhaps you think that you have nothing to offer the world. That you have no talents, skills, or that no one would want your help. It's not true! It is most certainly a lie put on us by the negative energy of the world.

Turn that around. Emit positive energy with strong affirmations. "I will find my purpose." Do not shrink back. Step forward in power. Just the fact that you want to have a meaningful life and build your life mission is a powerful source of positive energy that will help bring positive things to you and manifest the future you truly want. Physical ways that you can work towards manifesting are through a vision board and writing about your dreams and your ideal life. All of these will help manifest the kind of life mission you're looking for.

Building a life mission and finding your meaning and purpose is a noble goal. It can mean the difference between a lacklustre life and one full of fulfilment. And not only that, but you get the chance to make your mark upon the world, have a reason to get out of bed in the morning, and perhaps even make a big difference to the people around you. What a beautiful and rewarding thing that could be. Remember: everyone is different, and that means we all have different purposes and missions. Think about your values and skills and bring those to light to pursue your purpose. It's important not to compare yourself to others, for that comparison will steal your happiness, your focus, and your ultimate fulfilment. Be yourself and pursue that mission that is most meaningful to you and your life.

***

*There is a free resource available to download to help you use this journaling method. It will give you a visual display of how to get started. There are also several guided journals available for purchase that encompass these principles and your particular choice of focus. For example, there is a guided journal specifically for focusing on building your **life mission** whilst maintaining life balance.*

You can find samples of all our journals at
turtlepublishing.com.au.

Chapter Summary

To sum up...

- We all want a purpose or a life mission. Use your journal to build your life mission.

- Spend time in reflection. Think about your values and what is meaningful to you.

- Think about what you would like to do in the world and how you would like to make your mark.

- Journal about ways that you can achieve goals related to your life mission.

- Use affirmations to strengthen you as you take steps towards finding your purpose. Use manifesting to emit the positive energy needed to bring positive things to you.

- Don't be afraid. It's not about saving the world. It's about making small changes and working towards small goals. Find something meaningful to you and work toward that.

In the next chapter, you will learn how we can **put it all together**. This book has covered a lot, and right now, you might be asking yourself, "how can I possibly fit all this into one journal?" Have no fear; the next chapter is here.

CHAPTER ELEVEN

Bringing it all together

*"You just have to have the guidance to lead you in the direction until you can do it yourself." – **Tina Yothers***

It's about that time. Time to look back over everything you've learned throughout the book, start putting it all together, and get started. It could be a little frightening, but you've made it this far. That means you want to start making the changes discussed in this book, and you want journaling to help you uplevel yourself in all aspects of your life.

As we've mentioned before, you first need to find a method of journaling that works for you and your lifestyle, whether it's writing online, in a guided journal, an app or a simple blank journal. Just find a method. That's the very first step! There is no way you're going to keep at it unless you choose something that fits into your life seamlessly and makes you want to keep going back for more.

Before daily writing in our journals, we use the *Reflect, Dream, Bridge the Gap, and Decide* process for each aspect of our lives. This is a great way to kickstart the organisation of your journal. There is power in spending a little time reflecting and planning. How's your heart? How's your body, your mind, your relationships? What are you lacking? How can you reach your goals?

Now, it's time to get organised. Since there are various sections covered in this book, so should there be little sections in your journal. These don't have to be huge. It's a way to keep your journal balanced, and in turn, keep you balanced.

What does that look like? There is a free resource you can download to help you along, and there are a variety of journals you can purchase to suit your goals. Again, this is totally up to you, but picture a day planner. In a day planner, you'd write out all the things you'd like to get to that day, right? You might scribble in some notes about the various items. You write down times for appointments or deadlines. You might even look forward in your day planner and write down when things are coming up. While the journaling process is different, it's not dissimilar.

If you're used to and comfortable with using a daily planner, then think of a journal as your daily check-in with your life. Find a spot during the day, whether it's morning, evening, or whenever you can find the time. Think about all the various sections of our lives that we discussed thus far:

- Spending time on your heart
- Focusing on health
- Feeding your mind
- Working on relationships
- Building a life mission

Then, consider the tools you can use to fulfil your goals and create balance:

- **Using affirmations:** each of the above life aspects can have its own affirmation.

- **Manifesting your future:** either by creating affirmations to match your future dreams and activities that support your belief (for example, vision boards).

- **Gratitude:** express this daily for all aspects of your life, or those you feel need the most attention.

- **Other tools, methods, or activities:** each life aspect has specific actions that can support them (for example - meditation for the heart or reading for the mind). Consider which ones will suit your goals. You may also consider methods that fulfil multiple aspects at once (for example - exercise for your health and your heart or reading for your mind and your life mission).

One way to go about journaling through all the different aspects is to make a list and then go through and think of a quick action or activity that you could get through that day that would check off each section. Think of it as a

EXPRESS GRATITUDE
for what you
have now

HEART

REFLECT
Where are you now?

HEALTH

EXPRESS GRATITUDE
for what the
future brings

MANIFEST
what you
really want

MIND

DREAM
What do you really want?

EXPRESS GRATITUDE
for the process
of change

Create
AFFIRMATIONS
to support
who you need
to become

RELATIONSHIPS

BRIDGE THE GAP
What are you missing?

MISSION

EXPRESS GRATITUDE
for results
you expect

Create
AFFIRMATIONS
to support
your goals

MANIFEST
what you want
by making
a decision

DECIDE
What are you going to do?

HEART
Journaling
Affirmations
Meditation
Yoga
Self Love
Gratitude
Earthing
Reading

HEALTH
Journaling
Affirmations
Exercise
Nutrition
Water
Sleep Patterns
Breathing
Rest & Recovery

MIND
Journaling
Affirmations
Reading
Audiobooks
Courses
Education
Ted Talks
Podcasts

RELATIONSHIPS
Journaling
Affirmations
Phone Calls
Dates
Games Nights
Girls Nights
BBQs
Holidays

MISSION
Journaling
Affirmations
Vision Board
Contribution Projects
Planning
Manifesting
Goal Setting
Learning

list of goals for your day that focus your actions and help provide balance in your life.

So, for example, you could write something a little like this:

- **Spending time on your heart:** meditate for 5 minutes or spend a little time writing about how you're feeling that day.

- **Focusing on health:** 30-minute walk at lunch with a friend.

- **Feeding your mind:** spend ten minutes listening to a podcast at breakfast or on the commute to work.

- **Working on relationships:** schedule time for an important relationship (call your parents, go for drinks with a friend).

- **Building a life mission:** write a chapter of your new book.

- **Using affirmations:** select a few affirmations or even just one that is really speaking to you that month or that day.

- **Manifesting your future:** perhaps writing out your ideal day or looking at your vision board. It could be focused on only one of the aspects.

- **Developing gratitude:** write out three things you are grateful for (thread this through all the aspects of your life - grateful for relationships, for your work, for your current source of inspiration).

Can you see what we just did here? It's complicated and yet simple all rolled into one action! In less than ten minutes, we've made a plan for our day that ticks off so many important things:

- **Heart:** time for you, self-love, creating a moment of calm and peace in your chaotic life, preparing your mind for the day.

- **Health:** you've made time to exercise, which will help you feel happier as well as healthier.

- **Mind:** improved your mindset at a time when you would typically be non-productive.

- **Relationships:** made time for what's important amongst your busy day.

- **Life Mission:** made another step towards your 'big-picture' goals.

- **Affirmations:** built belief and confidence in your ability to live this life and manifest the future.

- **Gratitude:** reminding yourself to be happy for what you have whilst you work to improve your life.

Taking small steps every day to appreciate and nurture what is important to us while moving towards what we want more.

Tony Robbins said,

"If we want to direct our lives, we must take control of our consistent actions. It's not what we do once in a while that shapes our lives, but what we do consistently."

Take control of your journaling to create consistent habits that fulfil all aspects of your life. Success will come from repeating small habits every day. Direct your habits with the intent of reaching your goals.

Balance is such a valuable thing to have in your life. It keeps you from focusing so much on one thing that another area suffers. We need balance in order to succeed and make progress effectively. But it is normal to want to focus on one or two aspects more than others off and on throughout the year, so that you can really sink your teeth into them. This doesn't mean all your focus goes there, but perhaps you have a few more affirmations for that area of your life. Or perhaps, your time in manifesting is more focused on this particular area.

Let's say one of your goals is to make time in your day for exercise because your health is suffering as a result of your work focus. It's an important aspect of your life that needs to be addressed. Many of your affirmations could be focused on health or exercise, such as "I am committed and will take twenty minutes out of each day to move." Your section on manifesting could be focused primarily on health and how you can bring about the positive changes you want, such as weight loss, better sleep, sharper focus, etc., whatever your overall goal might be. That doesn't mean you neglect the other areas of your journal, but you may spend just a little bit more time on this one because it's very important to you.

Some tips to keep in mind as you bring it all together:

- Organise it in a way that is easy, quick, accessible, and fun for you! There are templates, but don't feel that this is the way you have to do it. It may take a bit of time, but finding the organisation style that you love will keep you coming back to your journal.

- Don't forget sections. Even if it's just a little bit of time each day, write down something for each life aspect, and you will achieve that balance. It's easy to get sidetracked by one or two areas, but don't forget to 'feed' the other parts too. They're all important!

- Don't discount the *Reflect, Dream, Bridge the Gap, and Decide* process. It is so important to get you started right, keep you focused and help you remember why you're in this, why you're doing what you're doing.

- Take a day off! That's right! There isn't any hard and fast rule about how much journaling you should be doing. Do what feels good to you. It does help to make it a daily habit, but it's also good to maybe take a step back and take a day off during the week. Personally, I like to use my journal from Monday - Friday for planning, Saturdays I take a day off, and Sundays are for reflection and re-organisation of the week ahead.

- Visualise the journaling process. Before you do anything, sit back, close your eyes, and think about what you want it to look like. This could change over time, but it helps to envision yourself taking the first steps. It's also great to visualise how the journaling process looks like for you because then you can find out how you want to go about it.

- Review and reflect on previous journals. Read back and see how far you've come. Has your mindset changed? Have you achieved goals? Often, we feel like we're not making progress until we are reminded of where we started.

Put it all together. Your journal is now an oasis, a place of escape for you to come and set goals, make plans, reflect, dream, and take steps towards the *future you* that has always seemed just out of reach. You will achieve balance by putting everything together and combining the skills you've learned in this book. Remember. This is a journey. There is no final destination when it comes to journaling. This is something that you can do throughout the rest of your life, for there is always room for improvement, change, and growth.

***

There is a free resource available to download to help you use this journaling method. It will give you a visual display of how to get started. There are also several guided journals available for purchase that encompass these principles and your particular choice of focus. For example, there is a guided journal specifically for focusing on various subjects like **gratitude, health, self-love** *and building your* **life mission** *whilst maintaining life balance.*

You can find samples of all our journals at
turtlepublishing.com.au.

Chapter Summary

To sum up...

- It's time to put everything you've learned all together in one and start your journal.

- We've covered the heart, health, the mind, relationships, life mission, using affirmations, and manifesting. Create sections in your journal to cover each of these daily.

- Every day, write a little bit about each of the aspects. It doesn't have to be much, but daily work means so much!

- You can focus on one or two areas more, but don't neglect the others. Balance, balance, balance!

- Make gratitude a daily focus.

- Find an organisation style that works for you; don't forget sections; don't discount reflection; take a day off, and envision the journaling process!

In the next and final chapter, we will cover **gratitude**. It's all about gratitude, and it's a great way to both begin and end. You will learn why gratitude is the most important part of journaling and how you can make it part of your everyday process.

CHAPTER TWELVE

It all starts with gratitude

"I don't have to chase extraordinary moments to find happiness – it's right in front of me if I'm paying attention and practicing gratitude." **- Brene Brown**

We know this is the final chapter, and we've stressed throughout the book that gratitude is an essential part of journaling. It is actually the **most important**. It is the beginning and the end, and everything in between. We could've put it at the beginning, but it's so important it may have been forgotten. This is why you're reading about it in the end. Everything we've discussed up to now includes an element of gratitude. Journaling for the heart consists of an element of being grateful for all the things that make your heart full. Journaling for your mind requires gratitude for what you have in order to create a more abundant mindset.

Gratitude is something so essential and yet often overlooked until we face tragedy in our lives. It's then that you hear the common phrases, "time is precious," and "be grateful for all that you have." Whilst a tragedy can be a reminder of reasons to be grateful, it should not be the only time it's given thorough thought.

Feeling and developing gratitude should be a **daily** exercise, and it will bring you a happier, more fulfiling life. Gratitude is the thankful appreciation of what you have, what someone has done, or of what is going on around you. A state of gratitude can bring you more than you realise.

An article in Harvard Health Publishing states,

"In positive psychology research, gratitude is strongly and consistently associated with greater happiness. Gratitude helps people feel more positive emotions, relish good experiences, improve their health, deal with adversity and build strong relationships."

That practically covers all the aspects of journaling we've discussed in this book! Gratitude is the ultimate key to happiness. That's why it's so important to include it in your journaling and in your daily thoughts and actions. But it takes time to develop, especially since we are all often prone to only thinking about and seeing the negative. It's easy to do and a common trap we all fall into. But if we can shift our attitude to gratitude, it will make the darkness turn to light.

But how? How can we tie gratitude into our daily lives?

- Write a thank-you note to someone

- Reflect and write down all the positives you love about your family or other relationships

- Focus your meditation on feeling grateful for all that you have

- Think about others in a positive light as you spend time with them, especially colleagues

- Make a list of things that make you happy

It sounds simple enough, and on paper, it is. However, the shift could take time, and it can be difficult to stop thinking so much about the negative, but you'll be happy in the long run. Working on gratitude can shift your focus onto all that is good in your life. It can be used for peace of mind in stressful situations. It can help you get over something difficult that's happened. It can also help smooth over those daily challenges.

Just imagine it. You could wake up each day looking at the world through your grateful lens. Instead of looking out the window, seeing the bright sun, and thinking how uncomfortably hot it will be, you can think about how lovely the sun will feel on your skin.

Instead of going downstairs to breakfast to see that your kids left their cereal bowls in the sink and complaining about it, think about how self-sufficient they were. They got their own breakfast. Instead of being frustrated with your boss at work and his micromanaging, you could focus on the fact that you know exactly how he wants things, and that makes your job a little easier.

These are all random examples, but they are small ways that gratitude can change your life. At the end of the day, you come home less exhausted and weighed down by all the negativity that surrounded you. Instead, you leave work and return home, having thought about the positive things that day, having focused on the brightness instead of the darkness. What kind of feeling would you rather experience?

We have discussed a lot of things regarding journaling in this book, but if there is one thing that you can take away, take gratitude. Make it a part of your life, your thoughts, your actions. Build it into yourself so that you become full of vibrating positivity and not dead weight negativity.

If you journal about nothing else, journal about gratitude. Spend time each day writing things you're grateful for in your life. In fact, you could simply use the five aspects of life that we discuss (heart, health, mind, relationships and mission) and be grateful for the part each has to play in your life. Without making any other effort in your journaling, this alone would begin to change your view of life and begin the transition for your mindset. Just imagine how you'll feel if each morning is spent in quiet reflection on being grateful. But if you want to do more, there are ways to include it in the journaling method we've gone over in this book.

In the last chapter, we discussed putting it all together in your journal: making sections and writing a little something about each section each day. Tack on gratitude! For example, if you're writing about relationships, and your goal for that day is to have a quiet dinner with your partner, jot down a little something that makes you happy about them. Maybe you're just grateful that they're in your life. Perhaps you love how they listen to you when you tell stories or how they ask you questions about your day. It can be anything! The smallest thing can make the biggest difference.

Similar to the *Reflect, Dream, Bridge the Gap and Decide* process, you could spend time at the beginning of each month (or more often) reflecting and writing in general about gratitude and what you're grateful for. Don't discount the small things, such as being grateful for the beautiful spring flowers! **No gratitude is worthless.**

For each of the other sections, add gratitude in, and it doesn't have to be a huge long paragraph. It can just be a little something. Something is better than nothing, and that's especially true of gratitude.

Chapter Summary

To sum up...

- It begins and ends with gratitude. Gratitude is the key to happiness.

- If there is only one thing you take away from this book, take away gratitude!

- In positive psychology research, gratitude is strongly and consistently associated with greater happiness.

- Journal daily about gratitude and make it a habit. Tack it on to each of the other sections as well for a more balanced approach.

We have come to the end. If you've started journaling along with this book, then you've gone on quite a journey thus far. In our **final words**, we will sum up what this book has offered you, and if you're still a little hesitant, we'll give you that extra little push you need to get started on changing your life!

Final words

You've made it. The time is now. You've learned the ins and outs of guided journaling and how you can use it to uplevel your life. Journaling is about connecting with yourself. It's about looking inward and dealing with what's inside there in order to make outward, lasting changes. It's about making a metamorphosis and changing into the *future you* that you've always wanted to be. It's about building a life of gratitude and happiness that has you waking up each day, excited to see what will come next.

It's now within your grasp. You have all the tools you need. The only thing left to do is take that first step. Some think that may be the hardest part.

In order to bolster your courage before sending you out into the world of journaling, let's take a look at all the topics we covered throughout the book:

- In chapter one, we focused on the question most people ask when they pick up this book: why even try journaling? On a basic level, journaling is just a safe space for you to be you. There's no one reading over your shoulder, telling you how to feel and what to write. You can just be **you**, and that's a powerful thing. It also helps you get out whatever is weighing on you, and you can find new insight from what you've written on the page.

- In the second chapter, we discussed the general overview of journaling - the types of journaling, the benefits of journaling, and the many reasons you can journal. Many people think that they have to journal just one way, and that way doesn't appeal to them. But the freeing thing is, (which is often repeated in this book), is that your journal can be anything you want it to be! It can be for any purpose that you want it to serve.

- Chapter three introduced the main focus for this book: the importance of balance. Life often feels like we're trying to stay on top of a surfboard amidst rolling waves. One wrong move, and we plunge into the turmoil, losing that balance that was keeping us afloat. Journaling can help you balance out all the various areas of your life, from work to relationships to your health. It helps you not focus too heavily on one aspect and neglect another entirely. Balance keeps you afloat.

- Chapter four related the value and strength of affirmations. These are a core part of journaling to uplevel your life, and without affirmations, it's like you have no base from which to proceed. Think of affirmations as the surfboard on the water. It's keeping you from drowning. Build your statements using strong and clear words that inspire you to move forward. 'I will' is how to begin and not 'I will try.'

- Chapter five discussed manifesting. It's all about manifesting these days. While it sounds simple enough, the practice can be difficult. To sum up that chapter, **you** are the key to the future. It's you who makes your life either miserable or happy. Bad things can happen to us, but it's up to us to react and build our lives in a way that makes us fulfilled. Believe in your future. Believe that you will achieve what you want. Send out those positive vibrations into the universe, and you will receive positivity in return.

- Part two gets us to the nitty-gritty of creating balance. In chapter six, we start with the heart. The heart is an emotional entity but also a physical one, and journaling is there to assist you with both! Studies show that the act of daily journaling 15-20 minutes a day can help reduce blood pressure - hooray for heart health! But as for the emotional side, the journal is a place for you to unburden your heart, release the negative weight that holds it down, and set it free. Journaling for the heart allows you to create a nurturing space, just for you, in the specific way you like to be nurtured.

- Chapter seven discusses journaling for overall health. Use your journal not only as a place to unburden but a way to reflect on work that you're doing to improve your physical health. Make plans, build lists, create steps that bring you closer to a healthier you. Your journal is the place for you to do that.

- Chapter eight. Don't forget the mind! Chapter eight covered how you can use your journal to feed your mind! Like your body, your mind needs nourishment. Not only does journaling give your brain a rest and a chance to unwind after the swirl of activity that is in our lives, but it is also a space where you can make plans to improve your mind. Reflect on what new things you're learning. Discuss the lectures, Ted Talks, books that have been on your mind lately. Give your mind a chance to feed itself, flourish, and grow.

- Chapter nine. Relationships are the reason we get up in the morning. We seek to love and be loved by others. We desire community. And yet, so many relationships (of all different kinds) fail or suffer because of a lack of time, desire, and balance. Use your journal to re-establish balance in your relationships. Take time to *Reflect* on how you can improve your relationships with everyone in your life. Reflect, plan, and even let go of those relationships that no longer serve you. Your journal is the key to helping you build, improve, and maintain your relationships.

- In chapter ten, we discuss purpose. It's driven into our DNA. You may have wondered what you could do in life, what would give you a purpose that would help leave a mark upon the world. That's where journaling comes in. Start thinking about building your life mission, what you want to see done in the world. It can be big or small; it doesn't matter. But finding purpose is another path to finding true happiness and fulfilment in life. Use your journal to plan your path to your life mission.

- Chapter eleven talked about how we can put everything together in our journal. There are templates that go along with this book, but you can also build your own. Each day, spend time thinking through each of the aspects of your life mentioned above and write down a little something about them, whether it's a word of gratitude, a plan to improve, or a step towards progress. Putting it all together will keep that beautiful, delicate balance alive.

- Lastly, chapter ten brings us to gratitude. Gratitude is like the glue that holds our journals together. As mentioned in the final chapter, if there is only one thing that you take away from this book, then take away this: practise gratitude. While the world can seem like it's falling apart around us, search out the little things that make you happy. Find the bright pinpricks of light in a dark world. Build your life around the good stuff and be grateful, for it will bring you happiness and fulfilment as you've never dreamed. Journal about gratitude each day.

That's it. The tools are now in your hands. It's now up to you to choose to step forward and begin your journaling journey. Now, if it seems overwhelming, don't simply throw up your hands and give up because it's too hard. Start small. Buy a journal, open an online document, download a journaling app. Then, start with a minute or two. Write down something you're grateful for. Write down a thought that's been on your mind. **Anything.** Get it down.

Then see how you feel about writing for three minutes, five, ten, and so on. Build it as you go. Start just writing, getting things off your chest, reflecting, picking out the positives in your life. Make your journaling time a safe and comforting area that you want to get to each and every day. Once you have the habit established, then you can start enacting the principles in this book.

Reflect, Dream, Bridge the Gap, and Decide. Start creating sections for each of the aspects of your life. Create affirmations, list your goals, build a vision board. Soon, your journal will be chock full of plans, hopes, guides, and dreams. It will be yours, all yours, and you can use it to push yourself further, to grow more, and to fulfil the things that you've hoped for.

Don't hold back. No change comes without work, right? It's scary and intimidating to start taking this journey inside yourself. At first, you might not like what you find. You may realise the severe imbalance that has taken over your life or the seeds of negativity that are holding you back from being who you really want to be. Work through them. Keep going. Keep up the courage, for there are thousands and thousands of others like you who want to make the same changes and achieve their dreams.

You are not alone, and you're strong. Believe in yourself, believe in the process, believe in gratitude, and you will bring yourself to new heights, new levels, and you will manifest your best life.

SPECIAL BONUS

FREE Guided Journaling Workbook to help you begin journaling using some of the techniques mentioned in this book.

Get FREE unlimited access to this AND all of my new books by joining our fan base!

SCAN WITH YOUR CAMERA OR GO TO
bit.ly/GuidedJournalingWorkbook

REFERENCES

Chapter 2

Hannah, Sharroncanter, Admin1, Laurindamahn955, Corinehardin537, and Maybellebennett. "Journaling Your Way to a Healthier Heart." The Heart Foundation. April 30, 2019. Accessed May 03, 2021. https://theheartfoundation. org/2019/04/29/journaling-your-way-to-a-healthier-heart/.

Chapter 4

Inam, Harun. 2019. "What Are Affirmations and How to Affirm Yourself?" Medium. December 3, 2019. https://medium. com/broftware-labs/what-are-affirmations-and-how-to-affirm-yourself-e079500c732c.

Dr. Carmen Harra. 2013. "35 Affirmations That Will Change Your Life." HuffPost. HuffPost. July 6, 2013. https://www. huffpost.com/entry/affirmations_b_3527028.

Corkindale, Gill. 2008. "Overcoming Imposter Syndrome." Harvard Business Review. May 7, 2008. https://hbr.org/2008/05/overcoming-imposter-syndrome#:~:text=Imposter%20syndrome%20can%20 be%20defined.

"The Science of Early Childhood Development." *Center on the Developing Child at Harvard University*, 30 Oct. 2020, developingchild.harvard.edu/resources/the-science-of-early-childhood-development-closing-the-gap-between-what-we-know-and-what-we-do/.

Chapter 5

"30 Powerful Manifestation Quotes to Inspire You." 2019. Through the Phases. December 15, 2019. https://www. throughthephases.com/powerful-manifestation-quotes/.

"How to Use the Law of Attraction to Create Your Dream Life." 2019. Through the Phases. May 29, 2019. https://www. throughthephases.com/how-to-use-law-of-attraction/.

Chapter 6

"Journaling Your Way to a Healthier Heart - the Heart Foundation." 2019. The Heart Foundation. April 29, 2019. https://theheartfoundation.org/2019/04/29/journaling-your-way-to-a-healthier-heart/.

"Highly Sensitive Person Traits That Create More Stress." n.d. Verywell Mind. https://www.verywellmind.com/highly-sensitive-persons-traits-that-create-more-stress-4126393.

Chapter 8

"Lifelong Learning Is Good for Your Health, Your Wallet, and Your Social Life." 2017. Harvard Business Review. May 17, 2017. https://hbr.org/2017/02/lifelong-learning-is-good-for-your-health-your-wallet-and-your-social-life.

Chapter 9

"Life-Saving Relationships." https://www.apa.org/monitor/2018/03/life-saving-relationships.

Chapter 10

Routledge, Clay. n.d. "To Feel Meaningful Is to Feel Immortal." Scientific American Blog Network. Accessed May 3, 2021. https://blogs.scientificamerican.com/mind-guest-blog/to-feel-meaningful-is-to-feel-immortal/.

Chapter 12

Publishing, Harvard Health. 2011. "Giving Thanks Can Make
You Happier." Harvard Health. November 2011. https://
www.health.harvard.edu/healthbeat/giving-thanks-
can-make-you-happier#:~:text=In%20positive%20
psychology%20research%2C%20gratitude.

Final Words

"Journaling for Mindfulness: 44 Prompts, Examples and
Exercises." 2020. PositivePsychology.com. July 8, 2020.
https://positivepsychology.com/journaling-for-mindfulness/.

Other resource links used for general research:

Morin, Amy. n.d. "7 Scientifically Proven Benefits of Gratitude
That Will Motivate You to Give Thanks Year-Round." Forbes.
Accessed May 3, 2021. https://www.forbes.com/sites/
amymorin/2014/11/23/7-scientifically-proven-benefits-
of-gratitude-that-will-motivate-you-to-give-thanks-year-
round/?sh=5eda5694183c.

"The 9 Best Guided Journals." n.d. Bustle. Accessed May
3, 2021. https://www.bustle.com/p/the-9-best-guided-
journals-19265385.

Koschwanez, Heidi E., Ngaire Kerse, Margot Darragh, Paul
Jarrett, Roger J. Booth, and Elizabeth Broadbent. 2013.
"Expressive Writing and Wound Healing in Older Adults."
Psychosomatic Medicine 75 (6): 581–90. https://doi.
org/10.1097/psy.0b013e31829b7b2e.

Ackerman, Courtney. 2019. "83 Benefits of Journaling for
Depression, Anxiety, and Stress." PositivePsychology.com.
July 10, 2019. https://positivepsychology.com/benefits-of-
journaling/.

Inam, Harun. 2019. "What Are Affirmations and How to Affirm
Yourself?" Medium. December 3, 2019. https://medium.
com/broftware-labs/what-are-affirmations-and-how-to-
affirm-yourself-e079500c732c.

"Affirmations: The Why, What, How, and What If?" 2014.
Psychology Today. 2014. https://www.psychologytoday.com/
us/blog/smart-relationships/201403/affirmations-the-why-
what-how-and-what-if.

"Why 'Manifesting This Lifestyle' Is All over Your Social Media."
2020. Greatist. September 24, 2020. https://greatist.com/
discover/rise-of-manifestation-mindset.

"BrainyQuote." 2020. BrainyQuote. BrainyQuote. 2020. https://
www.brainyquote.com/topics/

"What Is Grounding and Can It Help Improve Your Health?"
2019. Healthline. August 30, 2019. https://www.healthline.
com/health/grounding#the-science.

"The 10 Aspects Of Life That Matter Most". 2021. *A Conscious
Rethink*. https://www.aconsciousrethink.com/12892/aspects-
of-life/.

Available soon...

Journaling for a
Balanced Life with a
Health focus

Journaling for a
Balanced Life with a
Life Mission focus

Journaling for a
Balanced Life with a
focus on the **Heart**

Journaling for a
Balanced Life with a
Gratitude & **Manifest** focus

We will soon have a selection of *journals* available
worldwide as print or ebook at Amazon, Booktopia,
Barnes & Noble and all good bookstores.
Check **turtlepublishing.com.au** for a sneak peak!

Made in the USA
Las Vegas, NV
13 March 2022

45592160R00079